Towards the Learning Society

Stewart Ranson

CASSELL

Cassell
Villiers House
41/47 Strand
London WC2N 5JE

387 Park Avenue South
New York
NY 10016–8810

First published 1994

British Library Cataloguing-in-Publication Data
A catalogue record for this book is available from the British Library.

Library of Congress Cataloging-in-Publication Data
Ranson, Stewart
    Towards the learning society/Stewart Ranson.
       p. cm.
    Includes bibliographical references and index.
    ISBN 0–304–32770 — ISBN 0–304–32789–7 (pbk.)
    1. Education—England—Aims and objectives. 2. Education—Wales—Aims and objectives. 3. Educational change—England.
4. Educational change—Wales. 5. Education and state—England.
6. Education and state—Wales. 7. Motivation in education.
    I. Title
LA632.R36 1994
370′.942—dc20

93–43855
CIP

ISBN 0–304–32770–5 (hardback)
    0–304–32769–7 (paperback)

Typeset by Colset Private Limited, Singapore
Printed and bound in Great Britain by
Redwood Books, Trowbridge, Wiltshire

To John Stewart

Contents

Preface

In periods of social transition, education becomes central to our future well-being. Only if learning is placed at the centre of our experience can individuals continue to develop their capacities, institutions be enabled to respond openly and imaginatively to periods of change, and the difference between communities become a source of reflective understanding. The challenge for policy-makers is to promote the conditions for such a 'learning society': this should enable parents to become as committed to their own continuing development as they are to that of their children; men and women should be able to assert their right to learn as well as to support the family; learning cooperatives should be formed at work and in community centres; and preoccupation with the issues of purpose and organization should then result in extensive public dialogue about reform.

Such a society can only grow if it is supported by a framework of national governance that has, as its foundation, a strong system of local democracy that allows citizens from many backgrounds to play an active part in developing their communities, including the education institutions which meet their needs. Only such a new moral and political order can provide the foundation for sustaining the personal development of all.

While a number of recent reforms to the government of education may well contribute to the learning society, others can only frustrate its realization. The Conservatives' education reforms have sought to replace the post-war 'social democratic' tradition with the principle of the market place supported by power concentrated in Whitehall. Markets, however, will only fragment local communities, while centralized power engenders inertia. A better way forward will be to develop a system of governance that supports the purposes of the learning society, building upon the achievements of the social democratic approach as well as those of more recent reforms.

This analysis forms the subject of this book, which draws together and develops my writing on the changing government of education (see note, p. xi). At the centre of this work is an argument that the reforms to education since the mid-1970s can only be understood as part of the wider restructuring of the polity in response to the social, economic and political transformations which have been accelerating since the early 1970s. The response of both Labour and Conservative Governments has been to develop policies that brought into question the social democratic commitment to equality of opportunity and thus the post-war political settlement for a fairer society on which education, and public policy generally, had rested.

Education government and policy, therefore, can only be understood historically, in its political context, and subject to what Taylor (1989) calls 'strong evaluation'. There is no neutral, value-free account of education, the policies for which inescapably embody conceptions about what it is to grow and flourish as a person and thus necessarily incorporate definitions of society and polity that provide the conditions for individual and collective development. But the values of personal capability and social well-being that should shape education are not pre-given and will form a contested 'evaluative space', as Sen (1993) terms it. A learning society, however, will be one that encourages discourse about different ways of valuing experience and one that makes values responsive to experience. A theory of educational value, according to this interpretation, cannot be divorced from practice. While any reform of educational policy and practice cannot proceed without clarity of value and purpose the articulation of those values can be enriched and developed in the deliberative practice of introducing change.

The theorizing of value and policy developed in this book has grown out of engagement with the world of practice in local authorities and in schools and colleges. Whether in research or teaching or consultancy, my understanding developed most rapidly when I listened to the accounts of teachers, officers, advisers, councillors and governors about the problems they were facing and the strategies they valued for managing change so as to enhance the learning opportunities for young people and the communities in which they live. My work has been most influenced by educational practitioners who have been working in some of the most disadvantaged areas in the country, which have also experienced more than others the severity of the structural transformations of our time. Their radical rethinking of the values and practice required to fulfil the capacities and powers of the disadvantaged has been a particularly impressive exemplification of the learning society. What emerges is a revised vision of comprehensive education, of equality of opportunity for all, which builds upon the significance of institutional form and resource provision, with a perspective that the conditions for motivation and progress in learning lie in an empowerment curriculum and community development.

This book presents the first part of a project of theorizing the developing government and politics of post-war education. It offers a typology that periodizes the government of education and the political structures that underlie it. The analysis conceptualizes the structure and contradictions of political forms in each period and theorizes the role of transformations in the restructuring of the polity. Proposals are made for the restructuring of the government of education. The task of theory at this stage is to attempt to solve the 'problems posed by the historical process' (Bellamy, 1987). What is excluded, or left implicit, is a causal analysis that explains who the agents of change were and how they gained power to exercise their policy preferences. This will be attempted in a further stage of the theoretical project.

In developing the analysis over a number of years I have learned a great deal from many people in the LEAs, schools and colleges which I have studied and I am indebted to them for the support they have given to my work in research, consultancy and teaching. To many colleagues in higher education I have been particularly grateful for their willingness to read drafts and offer critical comment. The book draws together analyses which have been developing over twenty years in my work at Birmingham first at the Institute of Local Government Studies and subsequently in the School of Educa-tion. I have been very grateful to both departments for granting me sabbatical time to write and for the support which colleagues have given to my work. Throughout this period the encouragement of one colleague in particular, John Stewart, has been invaluable and in appreciation of the privilege it has been to encounter and learn from his relentless reflective energy I dedicate the book to him. He deserves better.

As always I am particularly grateful for the secretarial support of Jenny Neave, whose skilful work has immensely facilitated typing and word processing. I could not write without the support and commitment of Helena and our shared passion for comprehen-sive education. The book, with its attempt to recover a progressive vision of comprehen-sive education, is my small contribution to that project.

The evident flaws that remain in the writing despite this wealth of advice and support remain, of course, my own, reflecting the long learning curve!

Note

The chapters in this book draw together and develop my writing which has been published elsewhere:

Chapter 1	Ranson (1987), (1988)
Chapter 2	Ranson (1988), (1980), (1982)
Chapter 3	Ranson (1980), (1987), (1990a, b)
Chapter 4	Ranson (1980), (1984), (1982), (1985a, b), Ranson *et al.* (1986)
Chapter 5	Ranson (1988), (1993d), (1990a), (1991), (1992b – drawing upon an earlier draft with Bob Morris), (1993a, c)
Chapter 6	Ranson (1990b), (1992d, c), (1986) (1991), (1993b, d)

Chapter 1

Understanding the Crisis in Education

EDUCATION IN QUESTION: A BELEAGUERED SERVICE

Education in England and Wales has, for over a decade, been the focus of continuous review and legislative change that strives to introduce the most complete reworking of the service since 1944. These reforms, it has been claimed, would improve the quality of education and the effectiveness of government. Defining more clearly what was to be taught and assessed at each stage of learning would improve standards of achievement, while making schools responsive to more informed parental choice would create better and more accountable management. The reform of government and the reform of standards would go hand in hand.

The problems experienced by the service have deepened, however. While some of the reforms – for example, the need to create a national framework for the curriculum, or to focus more rigorously upon the quality of learning, or to delegate more decision-making capacity to schools – would gain wider support among the profession and the community, the package as a whole contains contradictions and confusions that render it flawed in conception and practice in a way that is now creating a crisis for the nation as a whole. The twin strategy of entitlement and choice as the means to quality always seemed to confuse the principle of universality (which extended the post-war social democratic project) with that of variety (the post-modern rejection of that project). Now each dimension of reform is collapsing in upon the other. The implementation of the prescriptive paraphernalia of subjects and tests is proving to be virtually unworkable; the strategy of encouraging competition between schools as the mechanism for improving standards is undermining the capacity of many to deliver the National Curriculum and to improve standards of education. The 1993 Education Act, by effectively removing the local education authority (LEA) from the government of education, creates the prospect of further bureaucratic centralization that will distance the service from responding to local needs.

The reforms accelerate an underlying decline. Underachievement, decaying buildings, impoverished resources and the low proportion of national income devoted to education compared with other leading European countries too often characterize a service that is crumbling, actually undermined by the framework of government that is intended to support its development. In his final report in 1990 HM Senior Chief Inspector provided a measured but daunting account of the problems confronted by the service (HMI, 1990). Mr Bolton censured the 'scatter-shot' attacks on education, believing that such indiscriminate fault finding could undermine attempts to improve education. He found much to applaud in teaching, including levels of achievement and increased rates of participation beyond sixteen. Moreover, there was no evidence that standards were falling and there were early signs of improvement following the 1988 reforms. He acknowledged, however, that nearly a third of 5–16-year-olds (two million children) were still getting a raw deal and that a third of all primary and secondary schools had been performing poorly (two-thirds of 9–11-year-olds were underachieving and reading standards were unsatisfactory in one in five schools). Long-term failings continued to confront schools, in particular poor standards of achievement among specific groups, especially inner city children and the less academically able. In the more deprived parts of the education service high proportions of children (68 per cent) leave at 16, having been taught in poorly maintained buildings and having experienced the poverty of resources more than others. There is a stubborn statistic, the Senior Chief Inspector concluded, of one in three children receiving a poor education. While any analysis, therefore, can point to improvement in the face of daunting resource constraints, the deep-seated problems remain.

Behind the controlled though pointed prose of the Senior Chief Inspector lies an emerging description (though not explanation) of the problem: the entrenched and interdependent pattern of disadvantage and underachievement. Thus it is not lack of capacity or educability of the disadvantaged that explains underachievement: it is more the conditions that have eroded the motivation to learn, or to take seriously an education which all too clearly has provided little meaning or purpose to their lives. If young people are failing they do so because society is failing them, withholding the conditions that provide them with the purposes for development and thus the motivation for learning.

An understanding of these effects requires an analysis of the deep social and political structures of our society which define the subjectivity, self-esteem and capacity of individuals and their communities. What this means for young people and the country generally can, moreover, only be grasped fully if the catalogue of decay is located in the wider context of the economic and social transformations of our time. The problems of 'a service' reflect a deeper crisis in society. For we are living through one of those historic periods of change that alter fundamentally the structure of experience: the capacities each person needs to flourish, what it is to live in society, the nature of work and the form taken by polity.

In such periods of change the well-being of society will depend upon the key institutions to support the present and prepare the new generation for the future. In our time this burden falls inescapably upon education, yet it is undervalued, while the purposes and institutional arrangements of the service are just not adequate to the task of the new age as it unfolds. Nor, as we are now becoming aware, can the systems in which we invested so much hope in the post-war years be adapted to the present purpose without radical revision.

Nothing less than a new vision of education is appropriate to the needs of the time, expressing the value of enabling capacity, not merely for young people, but for all within a learning society. The challenge is to support a richer conception of 'human flourishing' (the good, complete life for all) and of its source in the contribution each can make to the good of the community as a whole. For the person as a citizen understands that civic virtue and personal development are mutually reinforcing: 'the best polity', argued Aristotle, 'is that in which anyone whatsoever might do best and live a flourishing life'. The power of all can develop the qualities of each, but only within a more democratic polity that promotes public discussion in which the giving and taking of reasons is valued above custom, exchange and force.

The task is to renew education for all to meet the challenge of the time. New purposes will need to be supported by new conditions. Sustaining the springs of motivation to learn will in future depend upon the capacity of the public domain to establish the conditions for all to develop their powers and capacities. Such change will depend upon institutional forms of governance that can tie educational purpose to renewal of the public domain. This process of reconstruction can be helped by a framework that analyses the significant choices facing the purpose and organization of education in terms of the principles that organize the wider social and political order. For the learning society will depend upon the creation of institutional conditions that require building upon but go beyond the forms of governance that have shaped the post-war years.

THE SIGNIFICANCE OF EDUCATION

The significance of education is deep-seated historically, stirring those traditional sources of power – Church and state – to determine its purposes and forms; understandably, for learning can form a way of living. Thus, bound up with the way a society determines the purposes and opportunities of each new generation is an understanding of its own form and a conception of its future. Generations are time loaded. Because the arrangements for educating young people are arrangements for shaping their horizons and thus their sense of place, the institution of education helps to mediate the relationship individuals have to their society through social time and space. Thus the 'keying' of education, as Goffman (1974) might call it, tells us much about the emerging shape of the social order and its patterns of control.

The precise nature of education's significance has been 'essentially contested', however. For enlightenment thinkers such as Helvétius, 'l'education peut tout' and would create a civilized modern world guided by reason and knowledge. Others, however, have perceived a conservative potential in the power education. Illich (1973) can argue plausibly that education is the institution which most stupefies the masses and thereby subordinates them to the control of the state.

Such argument surrounds not only the likely consequences of education but also essential questions about who should receive it, what it should comprise and how it should be delivered. Those following the tradition of Plato define the purpose of education as one of selecting and preparing élites, whereas those pursuing the vision of Tawney (1931) or Freire (1972, 1974) promote the democratizing of an education available to all members of society. But what is that 'education'? Is it an introduction to society's most important forms of knowledge, or a training in the skills required in future occupations, or something to do with encouraging inner, personal, capacities to develop? There are choices to be made about the purposes and principles that are to inform education and these choices, typically, will reflect deep values and beliefs about personal development as well as about desirable forms of society and polity.

The diverse purposes of education

An education is multi-layered in purpose: its influence permeates society, economy and the polity as well as the experience of each individual. It can be the case that these purposes are compatible with each other so that educational aims in relation to individuals are consistent with the social or economic aims of the service. But strains can arise in striving to fulfil several aims that may be incompatible. I will discuss in more detail the diverse purposes involved in the institution of education before exploring the dilemmas that can arise and the ways they may be resolved.

Meeting the needs of individuals

During the 1960s it became fashionable to talk of 'child-centred' education, which made the development of each pupil the focus of learning and the centre of public policy in education. A child-centred education seeks to develop the personal qualities and capacities of each individual. To educate, according to this perspective, is to bring out, to unfold, to develop. There is a distinctive teleology underlying such a conception of education. Individuals grow and develop in a way that unfolds their inner potential. The task of education is to foster that potential so as to realize the powers and capacities of each individual. The learning process, by encouraging and unfolding the individuality of each young person, is designed to facilitate independence in thought and action. The keyword in child-centred education is 'progress': learning is evaluated according to the amount of potential achieved.

Educators committed to these purposes usually stress the process of learning. Learning, it is argued, is secured more effectively through experience than by didactic presentation of bodies of knowledge. Active participation by students in their own learning does more to awaken the imagination. Knowledge is rooted more firmly in self-discovery than in the passive reception of formal teaching. Students, perceived as maturing adults, are encouraged to negotiate their learning needs at each stage, drawing upon teachers as resources for learning rather than as omnipotent sources of knowledge.

The idea of a child-centred education, serving the individual needs of each child, came to influence government policy-making on the aims and purposes of schooling. The 1943 White Paper proposed that 'the keynote of the new system will be that the child is the centre of education' while the 1977 Green Paper *Education in Schools*, which summarized the 'great debate' on education, began its objectives for schools in a familiar way: 'to help children develop lively, enquiring minds, giving them the ability to question and to argue rationally, and to apply themselves to tasks' (Cmnd 6969, p. 6). The paradigm statement of child-centred education, however, was made by the Plowden Committee on Primary Schools:

> A school is not merely a teaching shop. . . . It is a community in which children learn to live foremost as children and not as future adults. . . . The school sets out deliberately to devise the right environment for children, to allow them to be themselves and to develop

in the way and at the pace appropriate to them. It tries to equalise opportunities and to compensate for handicaps. It lays special stress on individual discovery, on first hand experience and on opportunities for creative work. It insists that knowledge does not fall into separate compartments and that work and play are not opposite but complementary. A child brought up on such an atmosphere at all stages of his education has some hope of becoming a balanced and mature adult and of being able to live in, to contribute to, and to look critically at the society of which he forms a part. Not all primary schools correspond to this picture but it does represent a general and quickening trend.

(DES, 1967, para. 505)

Creative self-expression fostered by the 'informal' methods of the Plowden primary would not neglect the traditional virtues of the old elementary school – 'neatness, accuracy, care and perseverance, and the sheer knowledge which is an essential of being educated' – but provide a 'much firmer foundation for their development'.

Education for society: the transmission of knowledge, culture and morality

No one is an island. However much education attends to the particular needs of each individual part of the learning process, the leading out will focus upon learning to relate to, and to live with, others. In shaping the agency of the unfolding self, education necessarily shapes social relations: we develop ourselves in and through our relations with others. Education influences not sociability as such, but the scope of mutuality of persons in relation.

Education, therefore, cannot escape being a social and moral enterprise, encouraging ideas about the good of others as well as the importance of personal development (cf. White, 1982). Education carries the function of initiating young people into the moral categories and social qualities expected by society because the institution, typically, embodies a vision of the good society as well as the character and conduct expected of responsible members of society.

This suggests that an essential aspect of the education function lies in imparting to young people values and virtues, knowledge and rules, which it is believed they must possess if they are to become members of society. Learning, according to this understanding, is as much a process of shaping and guiding as it is of internal unfolding. For Peters (1973), being educated always involves being initiated into a set of values; for MacIntyre (1981), extolling the excellence of the classical city state, the good life for man involves not the self-centred individualism of modernity, but being educated to possess and to exercise 'the virtues' – of truth, justice and courage – that stand independently of each individual; for Passmore (1970), to be educated is to enter into the great traditions of critical and creative thinking. To educate is to acquire as well as to foster.

Education, therefore, typically has the function of re-presenting the values, knowledge and culture of a society to each new generation. This view of education, functioning to perpetuate the significant culture of a society, was articulated by the Robbins Committee on Higher Education (Cmnd 2154):

a function that is more difficult to describe concisely, that is nonetheless fundamental; the transmission of a common culture and common standards of citizenship. By this we do not mean the forcing of all individuality into common mould: that would mean the negation

of higher education as we conceive it. But we believe it is a proper function of higher education, as for education in schools, to provide, in partnership with the family, a background
of culture and social habit upon which a healthy society depends.

(DE, 1963b)

To be educated is to be introduced to the culture of a society, to learn its language, know
its rules of behaviour and acquire respect for its moral codes. There is always a socializing process embodied in education. Sometimes this can be explicit, as in the way
schools can function to reproduce the 'elaborate codes' of the middle class and thereby
the advantages of 'cultural' capital (see Bernstein, 1975; Bourdieu and Passeron, 1977).
Sometimes the socialization process can be more explicit. The most celebrated treatise
on education for socialization is of course Plato's *Republic*, which sought directly to fit
children into their proper places in the social and moral order: 'an account of education
which remains one of the *Oxford English Dictionary*'s paradigms for the meaning of the
word' (Ryan, 1974).

The Platonic notions of education survive. They make us aware that the culture which
is transmitted to young people in school can often be a selection of a society's values,
knowledge and experiences. If, as Lawton (1980) acknowledges, an important part of
education involves selection of the culture transmitted to the next generation, 'then the
crucial cultural question is "what is worthwhile?"' (p. 6).

Education for the economy: investment in human capital and vocational preparation

At different times since the Second World War ministers and economists have emphasized that the function of education has important consequences for the economy as well
as society. The expansion of education has been taken to be a precondition for economic
growth and modernization, because it can provide manpower with the relevant skills and
the knowledge to fire new technology: 'the formation of skilled and imaginative manpower is still seen as one of the major tasks of any government intent on socio-economic
development' (Oxenham, 1984).

In the 1950s education was conceived as an important form of investment. The
development of human capital was believed to be quite as important for economic 'take-
off' as new machines and physical technologies:

> in the mid 1950s applied economists discovered that earlier modes of capital formation of
> the Keynesian Harrod–Domar type could not account statistically for economic growth that
> had taken place in Western Europe and North America. This gave rise to a belief in a third
> factor in economic growth which was equated with human capital or investment in
> education.

(Williams, 1979, p. 129)

Economists began to focus upon the critical importance of investment in human beings
through education as forming the basis of economic success. In this country the case
for the economic rationale for investment in education was promoted with enormous
effectiveness by John Vaizey (1958) and by Vaizey and Debeaurais (1961). In *The Costs
of Education* (1958) Vaizey argued that 'a rising National Income required a more
skilled labour force to operate the economy and therefore a rise in the educational

attainments of that population while at the same time releasing the resources for under-taking that education'.

> The evidence for two propositions seems to be over-whelming: the individual returns to investment in education are at least as high as the returns to investment in physical capital in a market economy like that of the United States; and the social returns in all economies are also extremely high. Furthermore, the changing requirements of the economy for skilled manpower should guide educators in the kinds of educational structure that is needed and the content of the curriculum.
>
> (Vaizey, 1958, p. 7)

Vaizey's economics of education became extremely influential with post-war govern-ments. The Conservative Government under Macmillan accepted the argument of the Robbins Committee in Higher Education (1963) that a massive expansion of higher education was needed to provide the intellectual skills and knowledge required by a modern economy. Indeed, the Robbins Committee saw no conflict between the indiv-idual, social and economic functions of education: the educational needs of the indiv-idual and the manpower needs of the nation could be reconciled in the progressive expansion of higher education. Governments' manpower planning for economic devel-opment has focused as much upon the school-leaver as the university entrant. If young people are to make the difficult transition from school to work they need to be prepared with the appropriate vocational skills and attitudes. This continuing concern since the 1959 Crowther Report on 15–18-year-olds, the 1963 Newsom Report, *Half Our Future*, and the decision to raise the school-leaving age (ROSLA) announced in 1964* became an overriding preoccupation from the mid-1970s onwards. Prime Minister Callaghan's speech at Oxford in 1976 called for a great debate on education, expressing concern about the relevance of the service to the needs of industry and commerce:

> It was said that the school system is geared to promote the importance of academic learning and careers with the result that pupils, especially the more able, are prejudiced against work in productive industry and trade; that teachers lack experience, knowledge and understand-ing of trade and industry; that curricula are not related to the realities of most pupils work after leaving school; and that pupils leave school with little or no understanding of the workings, or importance of the wealth-producing sector of our economy.
>
> (DES, 1977a, p. 34)

The strategy of the Department of Education and Science to introduce a 'certificate of pre-vocational education', or the Manpower Services Commission in introducing YOP and YTS and then the Technical and Vocational Education Initiative, illuminated the intention of recent governments to introduce vocational relevance into the curriculm for 14–19-year-olds. This message was reinforced in *Better Schools*:

> A curriculum founded on these principles will in the Government's view, serve to develop the potential of every pupil and to equip all for the responsibilities of citizenship and for the formidable challenge of employment in the world of tomorrow. It is vital that schools should always remember that preparation for working life is one of their principal func-tions. The economic stresses of our time and the pressures of international competition

---

*The 1944 Education Act included provision for the Secretary of State to raise the period of com-pulsory schooling to 16 by Order in Council when satisfied that this was feasible. Sir Edward Boyle made such an Order in 1964 to come into effect in 1970/1; in 1967 the Labour Government deferred this until 1971/2 as an economy measure.

should possess the skills and attitudes and display the understanding, the enterprise and adaptability that the pervasive impact of technological advance will increasingly demand. . . .

In 1984, the Secretary of State . . . asked employers' organisations to identify those capabilities which their members look to the schools to have fostered in recruits to industry and commerce. . . .

The Government believes that the linking of education and training whatever form it takes should have the preparation for employment as one of its principal functions.

(DES, 1985, pp. 15–16)

The economic functions of education encompass investment in human capital and vocational preparation for future occupational roles. Education has always fulfilled another essential economic function of 'sorting young people into an order of eligibility' (Oxenham, 1984) for different positions in the labour market hierarchy. This selection function of education is deeply embedded in the structuring of the service: young people are classified, selected and processed by schools for entry to differentiated layers of the labour market. Although many believe the function of personal development should be preeminent, the ostensibly ineradicable function of education in practice has been selection for employment (Dale *et al.*, 1981; Hall, 1981; Offe, 1984; Dale, 1989). The determinant relationship between schooling and the labour market has been argued cogently by Martin Shipman:

education is geared to an advanced division of labour. This more than anything else determines what really goes on in schools, whether primary or secondary. . . . The pressure from the employment market comes through public examinations, entry requirements for jobs, and for further and higher education. It is the unintended consequences of this organisation to differentiate between children that is at the heart of this chapter. The school curriculum, the tasks performed by teachers, the rewards that accrue to them and the anxieties of parents over the education received by their children are all affected. The process of differentiation is institutionalised, built into education. It is rarely spelled out in a frank way as sorting out, selecting, promoting, rejecting. Teachers and lecturers would not acknowledge that sorting out is central to their work. Yet that is the reason for grading, for different curricula, teaching styles and lengths of schooling, for the variety in further and higher education and for the array of available qualifications.

(Shipman, 1984, pp. 157–8)

To acknowledge that decisions can be made which have such significant consequences for life chances as much as for the processes of teaching and learning indicates the inescapable political functions of any education system.

Education for the polity

Education is inescapably political and sometimes is used consciously to promote political purposes. It is because education relates so directly to the needs of our own personal development and because the form taken by education has such significant implications for the distribution of opportunities in society that the institution arouses such strong beliefs and potential controversy. The most explicit and articulate account of the political nature of education has been made by Kogan in *The Politics of Educational Change*:

Politics are those processes of discourse through which members of society seek to assert and ultimately reconcile their wishes. So those people who wish to make education non-political are . . . failing to understand that the purposes and procedures of education reflect what people want. It will be well to be clear as to how controversies about educational policies are in fact controversies about man's individual and collective present and future wants. . . .

Social policy generally never fails to incorporate ambiguity or conflict about underlying values. The tension between social needs and private wants, the balance between freedom and control between individual independence and collective efforts are present in discussion of . . . housing, social services . . . but because education is a desired artefact – its content and form are far more open to dispute than other social provisions. For these reasons education is political. It is volatile. It strongly reflects the open conflicting and wide varying preferences of a society which it also helps to sustain.

(Kogan, 1978, pp. 17, 20)

An institution that has such a pervasive impact upon the distribution of developing powers and capacities and thus upon society and economy is inescapably political in its functioning.

Education, through its shaping of individual and generation, can mediate the pace of social change, seeking to introduce new ideas and attitudes or to reproduce traditional patterns. Education can function to achieve complete change or Popper's (1945) ideal of 'piecemeal social engineering', of reforming society and polity gradually rather than through the destructive means of revolution. Thus the function of education in the post-war period especially has been to change society but to do so gradually. Governments have sought to use education to erode the barriers of social class and promote the sharing of language and culture, which are the precondition for a modernizing, socially mobile, society (see Gellner, 1979, 1983). Education in the modern world can function to create a more open, just, society:

Expansion (of education) can bring us higher standards more fairly shared. Education has changed society in that way and can do more. It does so slowly against the stubborn resistance of class and class related culture. But it remains the friend of those who seek a more efficient, more open and more just society.

(Halsey *et al.*, 1980)

Education is political not only because of its impact upon the distribution of power and advantage in society but also directly in the way it may seek (or not) to influence the polity. For many the function of education in developing citizens – willing to assume their responsibilities as well as express rights within the polity – is an essential condition for a democratic society. This interdependence of education and democracy was central to much of the debate that shaped the 1944 Education Act.

Education is political, in short, because it can characterize so many of the principles that underlie the social order. The openness, the opportunities, the horizons of a generation are embodied in the images and structuring of education.

DILEMMAS AND CHOICES

The importance of education, therefore, is illustrated in the diversity of functions it can fulfil for any society. Education can realize the powers and capacities of individuals, help to transmit language and culture from one generation to another, stimulate investment in the human capital required for economic growth and, by encouraging responsible citizenship, help prepare the way, gradually, for a robust and mature democracy.

The functions do not always sit easily together, however. The rigorous pursuit of one function may impede the accomplishment of others. An insistent preoccupation with the economic function of education, seeking to prepare young people with the skills and attitudes that will be required by their future employers, will probably divert schools from the function of meeting the personal development needs of each young person. Music and art may, under one set of priorities, have to give way to learning about business and technology. Furthermore, a concern to promote the culture of the past may conflict with objectives held by the polity to reform and modernize society. An attempt to pursue an extensive range of educational functions simultaneously may pose dilemmas for government of education.

The diversity of educational functions may often imply that a society will have to make choices about the balance of emphasis. The historical development of education in this country has often reflected the truth of this idea. In early Victorian England the function of education was the transmission of dominant culture and social control (Simon, 1964; Johnson, 1970; Grace, 1978). Elementary schools were required to 'educate' and subordinate an emergent working class: 'For Kay-Shuttleworth [the architect of popular education in the 1840s and 1850s] alarming disturbances of social order generally commence with people only partially instructed' (Grace, 1978, p. 11).

In the expansive 1960s the defining purpose of education – as illustrated in the Plowden Report – was the personal development of young people. Extrinsic concerns of economy or society would, it was argued, intrude upon the processes of learning and discovery. By the late 1970s, however, both Labour and Conservative administrations were concerned to emphasize the economic function of education above 'personal development'. The dilemmas posed for society by such diverse educational functions appear, therefore, to be resolved by emphasis and choice. Those choices typically reflect deep underlying values about the function of education and the form of society and polity it might help to create. The controversies surrounding the form of education desired by a society involve an argument about the priority which should be given to particular values. The shaping of education is the shaping of generation and society. The most articulate expression of these relationships has been provided by Williams (1961, pp. 145–6):

The business of organising education – creating types of institution, deciding lengths of courses, agreeing conditions of entry and duration – is certainly important. Yet to conduct this business as if it were the distribution of a simple product is wholly misleading. It is not only that the way in which education is organised can be seen to express, consciously and unconsciously, the wider organisation of a culture and a society, so that what has been thought of as simple distribution is in fact an active shaping to particular social ends. It is also that the content of education, which is subject to great historical variation, again expresses, again both consciously and unconsciously, certain basic elements in the culture, what is thought of as 'an education' being in fact a particular selection, a particular set of emphases and omissions. Further, when this selection of content is examined more closely it will be seen to be one of the decisive factors affecting its distribution: the cultural choices involved in the selection of content have an organic relation to the social choices involved in practical organisation. If we are to discuss education adequately, we must examine, in historical and analytic terms, this organic relation, for to be conscious of a choice made is to be conscious of further and alternative choices available, and at a time when changes under a multitude of pressures, will in any case occur, this degree of consciousness is vital.

Because education expresses the deep culture and political purpose of a society, choices about the service have appositely reflected and helped to reproduce the dominant beliefs and expectations of the society in a particular historical context: 'Education often acts as a kind of metaphor of national destinies. It seems to be a particularly appropriate vehicle for talking about the future of society in general' (CCCS, 1978). The structuring of education embodies a vision of what a society wishes to become over time.

ANALYSING THE CHANGING GOVERNANCE OF EDUCATION

The vehicle for the elaboration of educational aims as social purpose is found in the structuring of government, which constitutes distinctive values in policies and in its supporting organizational forms. This understanding of forms of government producing and reproducing a moral and political order derives from Weber (1978). A review of these analytical ideas can clarify the framework that shapes the ensuing argument.

Weber wanted to grasp the uniqueness of modern society while appreciating the similarity of social processes within different historical periods. For him all social forms exhibit a 'dominant order' of beliefs and values that legitimate the structure of power and organization. Societies reveal a distinctive pattern of power, values and organization. Power, the capacity to make people comply, is organized through appropriate forms of administration. But men and women obey typically not because of coercion, custom or material gain but because the organization and exercise of power are based upon consent and thus acquire authority. A form of rule is accepted because it is informed by a moral order that is perceived as legitimate. It is the legitimate authority of this dominant order of values and beliefs that provides a historical period with its distinctive character and uniqueness.

Weber was aware that the organizing principles of a dominant order would endure not only because they reflected shared ideal values embedded in appropriate forms but also because the enduring structure was sustained by and grounded in a 'constellation of interests'. The ruling order results in a distribution of advantage, status and power that favours some groups in society, who in turn strive to perpetuate an order that serves their interests. The fairer the distribution the more likely it is that the order will persist through time.

An emerging system of government, therefore, reveals a distinctive order of ruling values and interest that hold sway because men and women believe them to be legitimate. Power and organization are authorized in agreement about the form of rule. The elements of analysis can be set out in a simple model, which describes the constituting of a social and political order:

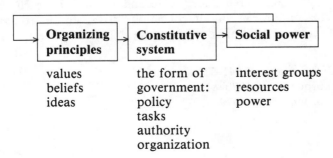

Organizing principles	Constitutive system	Social power
values	the form of	interest groups
beliefs	government:	resources
ideas	policy	power
	tasks	
	authority	
	organization	

The government of education is within this framework a structuring of power and values that embodies society's dominant beliefs about the distribution of decision-making. Yet those beliefs about the organization of power themselves reflect values about the form that economic and social relations might take in society. The organization of government, therefore, reveals conceptions about its role: in the relations between public and private, in promoting the common good, and in the development of the capacities and powers of citizens within the community.

A society that values the personal development of young people has historically created a more decentralized service so that teachers are afforded more discretion in interpreting their students' needs. Societies that value clear, simple and uniform purposes for education (such as preparation for economic roles) will tend to create more centralized systems of education (see Wilson, 1985). The values and chosen purposes decide, as Kogan (1971) argues, the nature of the educational task, as well as the appropriate allocation of responsibility and distribution of authority:

> government of education depends upon perceptions of who should be allowed to do what and who is capable of doing what. If teachers working with children are regarded as the prime agents in educational decision-making, the governmental structure will be relaxed or will even get to the point where it proclaims . . . 'the autonomy of the school'. If on the other hand, the educational system assumes that children are best educated through a series of prescribed tasks leading to a series of prescribed 'outputs' (rote learning of arithmetic leads to identifiable computational skills, for example), the authority structure will be such as to ensure that procedures, content and results, can be laid down by the system itself and are not the result of an individually created process between teacher and child.
>
> The ways in which different countries govern their education thus relate to the philosophies and practices predominant in their schools. Organisation relates to the tasks to be performed and to concepts of how the tasks can best be performed.
>
> (Kogan, 1971, p. 12)

Choice about the purposes and institutional arrangements of education will express the values and political culture of a society in its historical setting.

The organization of power and values embodied in government and the polity have changed in distinctive ways since the Second World War. The restructuring of education in 1988 or in 1993 as much as in 1944 reveals a similar objective, though informed by opposed visions, of social as well as educational regeneration. Distinctively different patterns of government have thus shaped the education service while the reforms of each new period have struggled with the influence of the past. Any reconstruction of the government of education will need to understand the past in order to prepare more effectively for the future. Indeed, it will be argued, any adequate future framework will need to draw upon the strengths of each period.

Three periods will be considered since the Second World War, each characterized by different systems of government of education, driven by different values and principles that reflect the interest of dominant groups. The periods can be summarized as:

- the age of professionalism, 1945–75;
- the period of corporatism, 1970–81;
- the period of consumerism, 1979– .

sufficient in number, character and equipment to afford all pupils opportunities for education offering such variety of instruction and training as may be desirable in view of their different ages, abilities, and aptitudes and of the different periods for which they may be expected to remain at school, including practical instruction and training appropriate to their respective needs.

(Section 8)

Moreover, the LEA was to have such control over the curriculum ('secular instruction'; s. 23) as was specified in the Act. Significantly, the initiative for change and development in local education was to lie with the LEA (ss. 11–13). Butler illustrated the point by talking of development plans during the committee stage of the Bill:

here we see the new machinery of the administration of education and this new machinery means that the initiative or enterprise, the variety and diversity to which we attach so much importance in English education, shall be provided at the instance of the local authority and shall differ in various areas, but that once the Minister has had the opportunity of approving the development plan and has made his orders, it shall be mandatory upon the [local] authority to carry out that plan.

(quoted in Griffith, 1966, p. 98)

Thus, as Kogan (1971) has suggested, there is much to commend the argument that the real say over the schools, the power to make or break an educational pattern, rests with the LEAs.

The LEA was charged with the duty to provide nursery classes and schools, special schools for the disabled and boarding accommodation to meet appropriate needs. The LEA should also 'secure adequate facilities for further education', including full-time and part-time education for people who have left school, as well as 'leisure time occupation, in such organised cultural training and recreative activities as are suited to their requirements, for any persons over compulsory school age who are able and willing to profit by the facilities provided for that purpose' (s. 41). The vision of the 1944 legislators is particularly revealed in their conception of 'county colleges' to be provided for: 'young persons who are not in full-time attendance at any school or other educational institution such further education including physical, practical and vocational training as will enable them to develop their various aptitudes and capacities and will prepare them for the responsibilities of citizenship' (s. 43/1).

The implementation of this section depended upon a date to be determined by 'His Majesty . . . by Order in Council', but this was never made. Nevertheless, this section, together with section 7, reveals of the responsibilities of LEAs charged with the vision of creating educated citizens who could contribute to the development of their community.

Just as the Minister of Education was not provided with direct control of the LEAs, so they in turn were deprived of absolute direction of their schools and colleges. Institutions were provided with a quasi-autonomous status under the general guidance of a governing or managing body, whose articles of government – determining 'the functions to be exercised in relation to the [secondary] school by the local education authority, the body of governors, and the head teacher respectively' (s. 17/3) – would be approved by ministers.

Ministers, local councillors, governors and headteachers were to be accorded their respective powers and responsibilities. And so were parents. Tucked away towards the end of the Act was a general principle of considerable significance:

In the exercise and performance of all powers and duties conferred and imposed on them by this Act the Minister and local education authorities shall have regard to the general principle that, so far as is compatible with the provision of efficient instruction and training and the avoidance of unreasonable public expenditure, pupils are to be educated in accordance with the wishes of their parents.

For their part, parents were charged with the duty of securing the education of their children by ensuring regular attendance at school (s. 39) and, more importantly, 'It shall be the duty of the parent of every child of compulsory school age to cause him to receive efficient full-time education suitable to his age, ability and aptitude, either by regular attendance or otherwise' (s. 36). Previously, parents had only been required to ensure for their children elementary instruction in the 'three Rs'.

By creating two strong authorities – central and local government – responsible for the provision of education and by leaving it unclear as to the nature of the relationship between them, the Act was implying that they would have to work together: and both with a third interest, the teachers. The key tasks, therefore, of winning resources, of planning and providing institutions, and of developing curriculum and teaching methods, came to be divided between three of the critical partners to the service: the centre, locality and institutions; between ministers, councillors and teachers. The 1944 Act thus created a 'complex web of interdependent relationships among the manifold participants' (Weaver, 1976). Whitehall was to promote education, town and county hall were to plan and provide, and teachers were to nurture the learning process so as to meet the needs of children and the wishes of parents. The constitutive system of the government of education formed a complex, 'polycentred' division of power and responsibility appropriate to differentiated tasks. Power was diffused between the partners. The upshot is what Briault (1976) has called a 'distributed' system of decision-taking and responsibility, so as to form a 'triangle of tension' of checks and balances. (Parents, it should be noted, though in law a key actor in the system, were largely excluded from the system of governance.)

The lack of clarity about the relationships, the absence of definition, suggested the need for 'partnership'. And in the post-war years much emphasis was given to the value and spirit of partnership. Celebrating a jubilee of the creation of a centralized department, the Ministry stressed the importance of 'the progressive partnership' between the Department, the LEAs and the teachers. The secretary to the Association of Education Committees, Sir William Alexander, affirmed the significance of smooth and flexible partnership in education.

Although there may be some consensus in the literature about post-war education forming a distributed system of duties and responsibilities, there remains more disagreement over the extent to which we may attribute power and influence to the partners. Fowler *et al*. (1973) talked of a diffuse, devolved system, while Bogdanor suggested that we cannot sensibly identify a 'controlling voice':

> the 'efficient secret' of the system, to adapt Bagehot, was that no one individual participant should enjoy a monopoly of power in the decision-making process. Power over the distribution of resources, over the organisation and content of education was to be diffused amongst the different elements and no one of them was to be given a controlling voice.
> (Bogdanor, 1979)

Some ministers at the DES concluded that their powers were very much circumscribed (see Weaver, 1979): thus Shirley Williams believed that 'there isn't much direct power in the hands of the Secretary of State except in a number of rather quirky fields; there is [however] a lot of direct influence'; and Gerald Fowler as Minister of State for Education agreed that ministerial power was constrained, although influence could create or change a 'climate of opinion'. This reinforces the conclusion of Griffith's classic study (1966) that the strength of the DES lay in the promotion of policy.

A number of writers, however, argue that, although the system of government in education distributes fundamentally different powers and duties between the partners, it nevertheless remains possible to attribute balance of influence and power. Within a decentralized system, it is claimed, the centre has nevertheless been able to retain a 'controlling voice'. Regan (1977) argued that the centre is the strongest partner standing in a relation of deep involvement to the service, although not in a relation of hierarchy or dictatorial determination. Other commentators are prepared to be more direct about the powers of the centre within the partnership. Saran (1973) ascribes to the DES various supportive roles, 'advising, moderating, pleading, cautioning and ultimately wielding the big stick of refusing its approval to any proposals from the LEAs which offend against national policy as interpreted by the Ministry'. Kogan (1975) concluded that the only ultimate certainty in the complex structures of educational policy-making was that the 'DES wields determinant authority and great power'. In 1974 a small team of investigators from the OECD (Organisation for Economic Co-operation and Development) was appointed by the DES to review educational planning in England and Wales and concluded that 'although the powers of government with regard to educational planning are formally limited . . . the central Department of Education and Science is undoubtedly the most important single force in determining the direction and tempo of educational development' (OECD, 1975).

There appears, therefore, to be some measure of disagreement among commentators about the distribution of power and influence within the educational 'partnership'. But the discussion is pitched at too general a level of analysis. Understanding of the distribution of decision-taking in education needs to be elaborated so as to explore how the balance of influence has varied over time – the attribution of dominance must be located historically.

Although it is appropriate to identify partners who have been more powerful in a complex educational system, I shall argue that the balance of influence and power has varied over time. The attribution of dominance needs to be located historically. Two approximate periods of influence can be identified during this period: a phase of administrative dominance (1945–55 roughly) and a phase of local dominance (1955–75), preceding phases of centralization to be considered in later chapters.

THE EARLY YEARS OF THE WELFARE STATE: THE 1950s

The early concerns of the welfare state were, perhaps necessarily, the creation of an institutional framework for economic and social reconstruction. The stress was upon the administration and provision of services for members of society in need. There was, therefore, a paternalistic and centralizing cast in the initial constituting of the welfare state: the state would provide for the needs of society.

Such concerns and assumptions were reflected in the structuring of government in the post-war welfare state. Decision-making was concentrated at the centre. Economic controls continued after the war, over wages, prices and investment policies, in order to facilitate the economic growth that would lay the basis for full employment. A programme of nationalization prepared to take into public ownership those industries that would become the infrastructure of the welfare state economy. When the Conservative Party assumed office in 1951, it accepted in principle a commitment to preserve state ownership of coal, railways and the Bank of England, to central indicative planning and to the welfare state (see Middlemas, 1979, p. 418).

The balance of influence between central and local government embodied and facilitated the wider state-structuring of power and values. The centre operated tight controls over finance and policy initiatives. Martlew (1983), in reviewing the development of financial relations between centre and locality, describes the framework of early postwar controls:

> after 1945 the long term pressure for increasing state intervention predominated, and this was reflected in the Local Government Act of 1948 which established the structure of central–local financial relations for the next ten years . . . increasing use was made of specific grants. Though a large proportion of these grants were distributed according to units of service or demand, there were also many percentage grants dependent upon local spending decisions . . . which were consequently subject to close central scrutiny and influence.

> (Martlew, 1983, p. 139)

In education, for example, there was sufficient scope for the ministry to exercise fairly detailed control over the spending decisions of individual local education authorities.

Planning the framework of educational provision

In the early post-war years it is arguable that the Ministry of Education was clearly the dominant partner. This can be supported by an interpretive account of the 1944 Act, which, it is suggested, intended to give the Minister directive powers. This interpretation is grounded not in a reading of section 1 alone (which, as we have already seen, laid on the Minister the duty to 'control and direct' national policy) but also in association with sections 11–13 and section 100:

- section 11 required every LEA to produce a development plan for the whole LEA;
- section 12 enshrined in the plan a development order, which the LEA had to follow and from which it could not depart;
- section 13 specified how an LEA could tinker with its system (for clearly there would have to be occasional changes) by submitting proposals to the Minister for approval;
- section 100 stated that the Minister would pay grant to LEAs directly in the form of specific grants.

Sections 1 and 12 were only meant to last a time, but they were about transforming secondary education. We talk glibly about secondary education before the war but the Act, through these sections, was the revolutionary change to introduce secondary education. Sections 13 and 100 were further key directive controls: 'Those who drafted the Act, which was to be the instrument of these radical changes, clearly saw the Minister as absolutely central to the educational system and gave him important powers to direct to other partners' (senior DES official).

Things did not quite work out as the drafters of the Act intended. A number of LEAs produced a development plan, but not a single development order was ever made. The reason lay in the rapidity of economic and social change. The gap between the world as conceived by the framers of the Act and the world as it was (with early post-war austerity, sluggish growth and a substantially expanded birth rate) began to grow. The world was too fluid, too under-resourced to allow the plans any overall relevance. For some years, however, this lacuna between plans and reality did not undermine the power and the influence of the centre in education. The Department continued to use the plans to monitor in some detail the development of individual LEAs while the control of recurrent expenditure of particular authorities through the specific education grant enabled officials of the Department to scrutinize LEA expenditure in detail and disallow particular items for grant purposes if necessary. Moreover, the Minister gave detailed advice through circulars, administrative memoranda and elaborate codes of guidance.

This strong lead from the centre was supported by two further factors: first, a broad consensus among the partners on education policy; and second, the strong leadership of the two main other partners. Bogdanor (1979) expresses the process of elite determination nicely:

> this process of elite accommodation reached its apogee during the post-war period when, so it was believed, any policy decisions in education were taken over lunch at the National Liberal club by a troika consisting of Sir William Alexander, Secretary of the Association of Education Committees, Sir Ronald Gould, the General Secretary of the National Union of Teachers, and the Permanent Secretary of the Department of Education. If these three agreed on some item of education policy, it would more often than not be implemented.

Two elements of this firm triumvirate partnership were significant. The first was agreement within each of the three corners. Alexander had no difficulty in speaking for the local authorities, and Gould, although head of only one of the teacher unions, was regarded as the leader for all the associations because there was no conflict between them at that stage – the manoeuvring for power had not yet begun. The second was agreement between them about objectives, which made the triumvirate easy in the early post-war years. The only argument was about how much money was going to be given. The agreed objectives were:

- eliminating the all-age school (reorganization at this time did not entail a debate about selective education but rather about getting rid of all-age schools);
- reducing the size of classes (classes were appallingly over-sized);
- expanding higher education;
- extending teacher education from two to three years;
- improving the physical standard of school plant.

As one senior DES official commented, 'these were not just agreed objectives, they were axioms, they were self-evident, absolutely taken for granted'.

TOWARDS SOCIAL DEMOCRACY: THE 1960s

In the 1960s some of the more radical ideas of the wartime 'contract to reform' came to the fore. They were facilitated by a period of economic growth and development. Rothwell (1982) and Mawson (1983) have described the central characteristics of the economy during this period. To the mid-1960s there was growth in gross domestic product (GDP) that comprised development in both manufacturing and service sectors, and increased investment led to the generation of new employment opportunities. New industries began to emerge as inventions and innovations of the 1930s in electronics, motor vehicles, aircraft and other fields were exploited. New markets began to arise, encouraging a stress upon product change and the introduction of new products. The end of the 1960s was to become a period of consolidation for the economy. It was a period of capital intensification, industrial concentration and organizational innovation.

With full employment already achieved, indeed taken for granted, and the welfare and social security elements of the welfare state gradually being put into place, governments felt confident in a climate of economic growth to begin expanding the services, which would, they believed, attack inequalities of the class structure more directly. Class division was seen as impeding economic progress as much as it offended to commitment to a just society. It was thus a period to realize more completely T. H. Marshall's analysis that the victories of civil and political rights starting from the eighteenth century were completed by the most important principle of the social democratic state: the rights of citizenship, the sharing of a common dignity, self-respect, culture and status within the community.

Citizenship presupposes equality of opportunity and influence. The expansion of education and community government were thus central to the development of citizenship within the social democratic state. Education was the key arm of public policy-making at this time. Greatly enhanced life chances through education would, it was hoped, provide the human capital to fuel economic growth, while increased equality of opportunity would support the disadvantaged and help to undermine the constraints of class domination, so facilitating a fairer and more open society. The organizing principle of education during this period was thus based upon personal development, extending opportunity, raising expectations and broadening horizons. These were considerable advances, though still guided by a limited, meritocratic vision rather than equality of material conditions and social outcomes (CCCS, 1978; Halsey, 1978).

Citizenship within a democratic state implies a sharing in the decision-taking processes of government. It implies a development of what Stewart (1977) has called community government, decentralizing participation to allow greater local influence upon policy formation, decision-making and implementation: 'decentralisation is an aid to social learning about complex social problems in so far as it points to a variety of responses to differing problems. . . . The aim must be to create schools, old people's homes, social work teams etc. as self-governing organisations within the parameters of the [local] authority' (Stewart, 1977, p. 16). During the 1960s a number of reports encouraged the involvement of local communities: the Skeffington Report on physical planning and the Seebohm Report on the personal social services, both in 1967, and the Weaver Report in 1968 on education.

This greater stress within the social democratic state upon the needs and rights of individuals and communities strengthened the role of local government within the state. Local authorities, with their potential for independent decision-making, clearly represented the devolution of power, was part of the social democratic spectrum of values (see Saunders, 1981, 1982). But it was as much the purposes of government as values in this period that determined the structuring of power. The commitment to education and new forms of planning community services required the locus of decision-making to be close to the point of action. Tasks and purposes shaped the organizational arrangements of government. The key actors in the network of government became local professionals rather than central administrators.

The social democratic state led to a period of extraordinary growth in expenditure on services. Changes to the system of central–local financial relations operated to encourage growth in expenditure. Martlew shows how in the Local Government Act 1966 the introduction of domestic rate relief was used as a mechanism for financing increased local spending. The centre also allowed interim increase orders to support the expansion of services as costs began to rise: 'thus, a conscious decision was taken to increase progressively the proportion of expenditure met from grants as the only way to meet higher local spending' (Martlew, 1983, p. 141).

Assumptions of growth, Stewart (1980, p. 15) has proposed, were deeply entrenched in the decision processes within and between central and local government: 'the allocation of the increment of growth came to be seen as the key decision'. These bids reflected aspirations for the growth of service within the public sector. Dunleavy and Rhodes (1983) have argued that such bargaining was the 'normal' style of central–local relations during this period. Bargaining reflected the belief of the time that the most appropriate mode of intergovernmental relations was that of consultation between 'partners'. Negotiations took place between the partners within a framework of consensus about the broad purposes of government.

Promoting comprehensive education

It was in the 1960s that the institutional conditions for equal opportunities really began to be developed and the key contradiction at the heart of policy began to dissolve. While the 1944 Education Act and the general thrust of post-war social policy favoured the creation of an 'opportunity society', the dominant paradigm of learning at the time, symbolized by the Norwood Report of 1943, *Curriculum and Examinations in Secondary Schools*, served to reinforce and reproduce the class-divided structure of pre-war society. However, the invidious selective system that labelled and excluded 'failures' began to give way to schools committed to a comprehensive education for all, the expansion of higher education opened up opportunities previously restricted to an elite and primary education promoted the child-centred learning that could deliver the promise of the 1943 White Paper, *Educational Reconstruction*.

The Norwood Report had provided a particularly clear account of the principles that would underlie the organization of secondary schools immediately after the war and that, for some, have provided a paradigm for the organizing of secondary education ever since. The Committee proposed that any age group can be classified into three types of child, each possessing a different 'mental make-up' of capacities and aptitudes and therefore requiring a specialized curriculum appropriate to those needs. This would be most effectively delivered, it was argued, in a separate institution that specialized in educating each type of child. Thus children 'interested in learning for its own sake' were best fitted for a 'grammar' school that would specialize in academic education, while children with 'applied abilities' would be fitted for a 'technical school' and 'limited' children with 'concrete' interests would be suited to a 'modern' school. Each type of school would prepare its children for appropriate destinations and occupations: higher education, the civil service and the professions; technical work; and manual labour in industry or commerce. Thus in the 'tripartite system', as it came to be described, 'the needs of three broad groups of pupils . . . should be met within three broad types of secondary education' (quoted in Maclure, 1965, p. 201). The allocation to each type of schooling would be determined by an intelligence test delivered at age 11 (the 'eleven-plus' exam). Although children were being differentiated into separate institutions it was intended that there should be 'parity of esteem' between them.

As the system developed after the war, very few technical high schools were established by LEAs, while some of the secondary modern schools began to offer examinations that were supposedly beyond their original terms of reference. Considerable pressure, furthermore, was building up from parents and teachers for children to have the same educational opportunities whatever school they were at. The psychological principles upon which the selective system was based were beginning to be eroded by research (see Simon, 1978; CCCS, 1981). The intelligence tests had no scientific basis, while studies increasingly illuminated the greater influence of home background and language development upon learning than heredity and genetic factors. The assumption that children's learning capacity was fixed and that any assessment at a particular point in time could form an adequate judgement of a lifetime's potential came to be critically undermined. Towards the end of the 1950s these pressures upon education to reform its system of schooling began to accumulate.

The vehicle for educational and social reform would be the comprehensive school, which would accommodate children from all social backgrounds and of all abilities, providing all with the same access to learning opportunities previously restricted to a privileged minority:

> The development of the comprehensive school over the last two decades has largely been based on the belief that educational advances and social gain would result from bringing together pupils of diverse abilities and social backgrounds. It is intended to offer not the same education to all but the same educational opportunities for all.
>
> (DES, 1977c, p. 8)

Anglesey, the first LEA to establish comprehensive schools, was also explicit about the purpose of comprehensive education: 'comprehensive education was not for the greatest good of the greatest number, but for the greatest good of all' (*New Society*, 1 November 1979, p. 200). The comprehensive school would be comprehensive in entry (that is, non-selective), comprehensive in age range and comprehensive in the curriculum it offered to all pupils. All pupils should have access to the same forms of knowledge and experience that would become the foundation of common life chances.

The comprehensive curriculum was, in principle, child-centred, designed progressively to focus upon the needs of each young person and to foster enquiring, creative capacities through individual discovery and experience. The influence of child-centred learning upon the internal organization of the school has been described by HMI. It led to:

- the abandonment of streaming;
- departure from the class as the normal teaching unit in favour of flexible groups in various sizes;
- team teaching;
- a move away from rote learning;

- formal subjects gave way to focus the progress of individual or group work sometimes on a project basis;
- aesthetic subjects and free expression were given greater prominence;
- a more relaxed classroom and school climate' (*Yellow Book*: DES, 1976).

By the late 1970s 72 per cent of secondary pupils were in comprehensive schools. Yet as Benn (1980) argued, 15 per cent of pupils in selective and private schools left the system significantly uncomprehensive. Moreover, it must be said that the process of comprehensivization focused in many cases more upon the difficult process of establishing comprehensive schools on the basis of reorganized grammar and secondary modern schools than upon the internal development of the learning process.

Although education typically invokes strongly articulated political values, for example about the rights of parents to determine their children's education, or about the justice of equal opportunities for personal development, the period from the mid-1950s to the mid-1960s saw an unusual period of agreement between the major political parties about the importance, purposes and organization of education. Kogan (1978) describes this phase of consensual politics in the government of education:

> The consensus period was essentially one when Conservative Ministers such as David Eccles and Edward Boyle inherited the new conservatism forged in the Conservative Research Centre by Iain Macleod under the aegis of liberal conservatives such as R. A. Butler. During the Macmillan period in British politics, Conservatives were prepared to regard an improvement of public services as part of the rewards that an opportunity state could offer to its consumers.

Labour's willingness, when it issued Circular 10/65, to 'request' LEAs to prepare for comprehensive reorganization of schools, rather than impose the changes on authorities, illustrated its commitment to consensus politics: letting change evolve rather than imposing radical change. The consensus lasted as long as policies centred upon equalizing opportunities. Once Labour, advised by Anthony Crosland, began to articulate a stronger notion of equality in education and in later administrations began to legislate (for example, the 1970 Education Act) for the implementation of reorganization, then the consensus began to dissolve.

Shifting balance of power

The emphasis upon the education of individual pupils reinforced the original bias to decentralization within the system. Only the professional judgement of teachers in the classroom could identify the learning needs of each pupil, and release his or her talents and capacities. Other partners needed to support this fragile relationship. Young citizens had to be nurtured in a caring environment by professionals dedicated to public service.

The balance of power began to shift as the years passed and the local authorities gained power at the expense of the centre. Studies showed that there was enormous scope for LEA autonomy and discretion:

> not only on matters of style – for example, type of secondary education provided, the content of the curriculum and the age of transfer from primary . . . but also in terms of the amount of resources used in the education service, for example, teaching staff, age and standard of buildings, equipment and facilities.
>
> (Pyle, 1976)

Ironically, in view of the LEAs' opposition, it was that change in the arrangements for central grant which most loosened the central hold. In 1958 the grant-funding arrangements changed with the introduction of General Grant (later to be superseded by Rate Support Grant), ending the close scrutiny by the Department of LEA recurrent expenditure. The centre also ceded detailed control of capital expenditure. Guidance, in the form of circulars and administrative memoranda, also became less detailed.

It is in studies of comprehensive secondary reorganization that the shifting balance of power becomes clearly apparent. First, the initiatives were often made by local rather than central government:

> in fact a number of LEAs had either reorganised or were seriously considering doing so well before central government was committed to such a course of action. Indeed until 1965 the role of central government whether Labour or Conservative controlled, was usually to inhibit and delay local initiative in the area. . . . When national government introduced its own plans in the mid-sixties it drew heavily on the experience of those authorities.
>
> (James, 1980)

Second, LEAs were able to negotiate considerable discretion to suit local circumstances. Third, the LEA had the ability to win out in a test of power – that is, to achieve objectives in the face of opposition and resistance.

The cases of Tameside and Enfield illustrate the ability of an LEA (in the case of the former authority) and a local action group (in the case of the latter authority) to frustrate the intentions of the Secretary of State in the courts and win. In short, the attempt to promote comprehensive schools illustrated the essential weakness of the centre when confronted with resolute opposition. The financial and educational changes discussed above demonstrate the diminishing power of the centre in this period. A number of other, broadly political, factors also contributed to the process over time. First, the teacher unions became more militant in pursuit of their professional claims (see Coates, 1972). Second, the rapid growth of political organization and of corporate management in many local authorities contributed to an increase in the centralization and concentration of decision-making so that the dialogue that central departments, such as the DES, had with local services came increasingly to be mediated by the local authority in general at a political and an official level. Third, the voice of the consumer came to be articulated more clearly and vociferously. The body politic of education in particular and local government in general became more organized and aggressive in pursuit of sectional claims. But, at the same time, it became more fragmented and therefore more difficult for the centre to connect with and control.

The policy planning processes

The policy planning process reflected and was coterminous with the general division of functions, duties and responsibilities. Curriculum and teaching method remained largely under the planning control of teachers in schools, the establishment, staffing and maintenance of institutions were the planning responsibilities of LEAs, and the planning of the broad framework of policy and resources was done centrally. There was no specialized planning function anywhere within the service. The general consensus about policy was publicly debated and formulated in the period's great central Advisory Councils (Crowther, Newsom, Robbins, Plowden, etc.), which left the troika, as

Bogdanor (1979) calls them, merely to discuss the winning of resources and matters of timing.

The processes of policy planning, therefore, were largely incremental, building on what had been accomplished and making discrete improvements to the inherited quality of the service. There was no system of comprehensive, programmatic analysis and review of need and achievement. The scope of planning was limited, the nature of the change contemplated was gradual. As one official commented, 'planning in this period was just *ad hoc* . . . there was no continuous planning'. The complexities, uncertainties, and necessary time lags in planning for the service encouraged a more leisurely pace to the introduction of change and a highly flexible, *laissez-faire* approach to planning for change.

Access to educational planning varied. The determination of general policy by the great Advisory Councils was a form of, albeit élite, public participation, with the notables from different parts of the education network meeting to shape meanings, purposes and policies that should underpin the development of the service. Their reports became public documents and would be the subject of public debate and analysis in conference halls and seminar rooms, in council chambers and meeting rooms. The education service was conceived as a national service and the attachment to the service was public and had an important dimension of openness, although access to the policy-making councils was determined by informal processes of influence in the network. Timing and implementation of national policy at the outset of the period were a more closed affair of élite determination, though by the close the initiative lay firmly with the LEAs and the teachers. Education began to reach out to its public and consult them about proposals for comprehensive reorganization; but consultation was usually only at a level of providing information.

Policy planning in education at this stage lacked an integrated structure and formal rationality in its processes. Relations in the planning network were characterized by consensus, informality and intermittent bargaining. And the relations of power in the network? The balances of power and dependence favoured those partners at the level of the locality in the educational network: the teachers and, in particular, the LEAs. They were able to expand their power and discretion because they monopolized the ownership of critical resources that were unavailable elsewhere while possessing the sanctions necessary to reinforce such scarcity. The teachers owned the most valued professional expertise required to give effect to a curriculum designed to fulfil diverse individual needs. To underpin this critical resource the teachers organized, inserted themselves at all levels of the decision-making process and increasingly undertook militant sanctions that were effective in winning concessions to economic and professional goals (Coates, 1972; Locke, 1974). The LEAs, for their part, were able to consolidate and expand their area of discretion, by possession of the legal resource of 'gatekeeper', to policy implementation as well as alternative sources of finance (in many cases) should the centre take retributive action. The LEA could, if it chose, remain indifferent to the values of a centrally defined partnership and, if necessary, impose its own sanctions on government: delay central initiatives, deny information and ultimately claim redress in the courts. When necessary the teachers and the LEAs, as Archer (1979) nicely describes, exchanged alliances to reinforce localist causes and frustrate the centre: 'the NUT and the AEC played a mutually supportive role in protecting their extensive autonomous powers of decision-making'.

The education system at this stage in its development may be summarized by its lack of systemic qualities: differentiated, decentralized, diffuse, non-formal, non-programmatic. The education sector possessed some of the characteristics of what anthropologists call a segmentary form of social organization, lacking any political centralization, formal hierarchy of authority or pattern of social stratification. Relatively independent but complementary social units 'nested' within each other (see Gellner, 1969, 1981). The interest of segmentary social forms lies in the way they achieve any social cohesion in the absence of effective central institutions or strong leadership. The pervasive threat of violence, mediated by charismatic saints, has often fulfilled the function of maintaining social integration in such societies.

The threat of disorder and chaos within education (with 30,000 relatively autonomous institutions pursuing their own interests, which became a concern for the DES in the period of corporatism) was averted by two significant mechanisms. First, consensus about the values and purposes that should shape the service acted as a major instrument of social cohesion, legitimated by the education world's charismatic saints (for example, Robbins and Plowden), whose extraordinary ideas and qualities served to afford leadership and inspiration where formerly they were absent. Second, accelerated expansion of the service provided the financial resources to pursue the saintly ideas and, more importantly, enabled disparate sectional interests to cohere.

Within a few years (by the mid-1970s) the segmented education network had lost its two mechanisms of social cohesion, common ideals and abundant resources. Bereft of its comfortable means of cohesion, education would need to search for alternative forms of integration.

CONCLUSION

During the 1960s and early 1970s the education service enjoyed a period of unrivalled growth and privilege. A rising birth rate, economic growth and, most importantly, political will for social reform coalesced in the expansion of education. To accomplish these great expectations fundamental changes were planned for institutions and the curriculum. The old outmoded tripartite school system, which selected and excluded the majority of young people, was remodelled in favour of comprehensive schools that would impose no artificial barriers on the development of pupils. All would then have access to the same forms of knowledge and experience that would became the foundation of common life chances. The curriculum was designed progressively to focus upon the needs of each young person and to foster enquiring, creative capacities through individual discovery and experience. The focus was upon personal development rather than preparation for future economic and vocational roles. The education system adjusted to such purposes and tasks, with considerable influence accorded to the key community of professional teachers in schools and to the LEA as the strategic planning agency. A strong boundary differentiated education and its profession from the lay environment.

Policy and planning processes were largely incremental, building upon what had been accomplished. The widespread consensus about policy had been debated publicly and formulated in the period's great Advisory Councils, which incorporated notable representatives of the profession and public as well as central and local government.

Given a framework of policy, planning became a matter of timing and winning resources. There was no system of comprehensive, programmatic analysis and review of need and achievement. The role of the Department was responsive, incremental and resource-oriented.

In short, if the code of the system was that of opportunity, of raising expectations, of lifting horizons, then the key to the system was provided largely by professional actors – the LEAs and the teachers – sharing beliefs in a decentralized polycentric system of administration and planning.

Chapter 3

The Transformations of Our Time

No sooner had many LEAs implemented a scheme of comprehensive education in the 1960s or early 1970s than they were forced to contemplate a further period of reorganizing their schools and colleges. By the late 1970s a number of LEAs began to appreciate the scale of demographic change implied in the falling birth rate and its likely effect upon their school rolls. For some, the prospect was that by 1990 they would not have enough pupils to fill half their existing schools. The issue of what to do with 'surplus capacity' in schools generated controversies in the service, but how these were defined often reflected the perspectives taken on the wider economic and social transformations that were beginning to have their impact on society and polity.

THE CHANGING CONTEXT OF EDUCATION

Education had been the fastest-growing service – whether in the public or the private sector – between 1955 and 1975 (Cheshire, 1976). A rising birth rate, economic growth and political will coalesced in the expansion of the education service during that period. After the Second World War, LEAs had to build more schools to provide for the growing school population. But the same forces that led to the expansion of education turned, from the mid-1970s, into forces of contraction. A declining birth rate and the prospect of falling school rolls, the economic recession and the ensuing public expenditure cuts, together with growing disquiet about the achievement of the service, all combined to produce a more severe context for education.

Falling school rolls

The birth rate fell by about one-third between 1964 and 1977. The implications for the numbers of pupils in school were dramatic: the school population, which grew to a peak of nine million in 1977 (from five million in 1946), was anticipated to decline perhaps to below seven million by 1990. Primary school numbers peaked in 1973, then fell by about 30 per cent before beginning to rise again in the mid-1980s, while secondary numbers peaked in 1980 at 4.1 million and would fall to 2.8 million in 1991. Although it was known that the birth rate would increase again, demographic predictions in the early 1980s did not anticipate rapid growth or, therefore, the prospect of great increases in school rolls before the next century was well advanced.

LEA planners, moreover, could not expect the spare places in their schools to be filled with increasing numbers of young people deciding to stay on into the sixth form. In the late 1970s, the 'staying on rate' was relatively static or even falling, while those choosing to go to further education colleges were increasing and, as youth unemployment grew, those young people who used to leave school for work were choosing to (or were constrained to) join the new training schemes rather than stay on into the sixth form.

Expenditure cuts

The recession caused by the 1973 oil price rises led in due course to rolling programmes of cuts in public expenditure and local authority spending in particular. The elaborate machinery of expenditure controls on local authorities – targets, rate caps, penalties and so on – was designed necessarily to reduce education (60 per cent of local government expenditure) as well as other social services. When Peston (1982) and Stewart (1984) analysed the value of rate support grant in real terms (what money will buy taking into account inflation) they revealed substantial cuts in allocated expenditure. The constraints on local government expenditure grew more severe in the 1980s.

Year by year HM Inspectorate, in its annual reports on the effects of expenditure policies on education, illustrated the impacts of cuts: 'many schools are finding it increasingly difficult to replace old books, equipment and furniture, to implement curricular change, and to respond to planned changes in assessment and examination procedures' (HMI, 1986). This toll of cuts on the learning experiences of young people in schools was graphically chronicled in Hewton's (1986) *Education in Recession*. He found, in a study on one shire county, that there had been severe cutbacks at all levels in the school system, with implications for morale and the quality of teaching.

The Conservative Government claimed, properly, that educational spending per pupil had risen since it took power in 1979. The implied contradiction between cuts and growth can be understood, however, if the assumptions upon which government based its grant were made explicit. The government's expenditure plans assumed that local authorities had removed 'surplus' provision (i.e. teachers) and capacity (i.e. school places). But most LEAs had often not wanted, or been able, either to close schools or to reduce their teaching forces at the pace required to show an 'efficient' relationship between finance and provision. Cuts in other areas of expenditure, therefore, were inescapable. The need to cut has also been reinforced by the higher rate of inflation among educational goods and services.

The necessity of change

It is possible, though unlikely, that if rolls alone had changed the service could have adjusted without altering its forward stride. But the juxtaposition of so many elements of transformation and challenge meant that change in the way the service operated was inevitable. As Dudley Fiske (1978), the former Chief Education Officer of Manchester, perceived at the time, 'no change was not an option'. What action should follow to deal with the surplus capacity that arose from falling school rolls was, however, a contentious issue and gave rise to a number of questions and controversies.

The first set of questions focused upon major *issues of public policy*: what should be done with the spare capacity in schools created by falling rolls? Economic values of efficient use of public resources suggested an urgent need to rationalize surplus places in order to release scarce public funds for alternative uses – perhaps for the elderly and their growing need for care and sheltered accommodation. Value for money suggested a programme of school closure and amalgamation. Yet political values, on the other hand, could suggest that spare capacity might provide an opportunity for parents to exercise their right to choose a school. This would also strengthen the public accountability of schools. The competing claims of rationalization and parental choice generated a growing controversy.

Falling rolls raised questions about a number of *educational policies*. The local education authority would have to review its commitment to the values of providing educational opportunities to all young people. It would have to ask what curriculum should be offered in each school to support such opportunities and what size of school was needed to justify the staffing of this curriculum. These questions required an LEA to consider whether the quality of education provided in any individual school depended upon managing all the schools as an interdependent system. Further questions about education policy focused upon the organization of learning and asked: What kind of school will provide the best education for its pupils? Should schools remain 'comprehensive'? Should schools retain small ('uneconomic') sixth forms? Could post-16 education in schools and colleges be rationalized? Does a good education depend upon separating out kinds of learning between different types of institution or integrating the curricular opportunities, especially for young adults?

A third and connected set of questions raised by falling rolls and institutional change has been about decision-making procedure. There has been concern over how decisions are arrived at as well as what they are. These are *questions about government* and public administration. What form of decision-making would result in the best education for young people? Would greater central control enhance efficiency, speed up change and ensure accountability, or would centralization be detrimental to realizing these objectives of public policy?

Such deep questions were reinforced by the impact of transitions in the structural context of education.

THE WIDER TRANSFORMATIONS

The demographic and financial changes facing education reflected dimensions of a much broader series of transformations that were changing the face of society. These have been many-sided – social, economic and political, often quite independent of each other – yet together they combined to alter fundamentally the world we had become accustomed to and established new agendas for the polity. Understanding these changes is a precondition for interpreting the agendas for educational reform. The economic, social and political changes will be discussed in turn.

The long post-war period of economic growth and prosperity in Britain came to an end with the 1973 oil crisis. The Western economies had been faltering since the late 1960s, bolstered by expansive monetary and fiscal policy, but the OPEC decision to raise oil prices and the embargoing of oil to the West during the Arab–Israeli war precipitated a recession among the Western economies more severe than anything experienced since the 1930s. Stagnant production combined with increasing inflation to undermine competitiveness in international markets, and led inexorably to balance of payment deficits and currency depreciation. The recession, together with the contraction of production, caused accelerating unemployment, with over three million registered as unemployed in the early 1980s and with the adviser to the House of Lords Select Committee on Unemployment, Daniels (1980), acknowledging that real levels of unemployment were underestimated by over one million. (Thirty million people were unemployed at this time in the OECD countries.) In the West Midlands a decline of 16 per cent in employment from 1980 to 1983 represented the greatest percentage loss of any region in Britain. This story seemed to narrate the collapse of Britain's manufacturing heartland.

The contraction of metal manufacturing and heavy industry in general prompted some to talk of an incipient process of 'deindustrialization' (e.g. Weiner, 1981) within the first industrial nation. Others have spoken of the restructuring of capitalism (see Offe, 1985; Lash and Urry, 1987). Massey and Meegan (1982) produced a powerful account of the mechanisms of industrial intensification, rationalization and technical innovation that lead to the ensuing anatomy of job loss and human redundancy. Most of 'the shake out' of surplus labour had been caused by the first two processes but the trend was set towards an accelerating implementation of the information revolution produced by microelectronic and computer technologies and thus a further substitution of capital for labour. For Harvey (1989, p. 145) these changes have exemplified the response of industrial conglomerates to the squeeze on their profitability:

> Technological change, automation, the search for new product lines and market niches, geographical disperal to zones of easier labour control, mergers, and steps to accelerate turnover time of their capital surged to the fore of corporate strategies for survival under general conditions of deflation.

Harvey and others (e.g. Hall and Jacques, 1989; Murray, 1989) argue that these strategies for regenerating the competitiveness of capital have taken such a distinctive form that they have inaugurated a new era of capitalism. Profitability has been restored by the introduction of more flexible forms of production, labour market segmentation and organizational arrangement. These forms of 'flexible accumulation' have been termed *post-Fordist* to distinguish them from the type of mass production of standardized goods pioneered by Henry Ford, which became the paradigm for industrial development in the post-war world and the rigidities of which prevented its smooth adaptation to a changed context. The flexible firm develops a capacity to 'customize' its business, designing quality goods and services to meet the needs and changing fashions of diverse groups (or 'niches') in the market place. Firms develop flexible production systems to respond to and exploit the changing whims of fashion in more specialized markets, including small-batch production, subcontracting, and core and peripheral (casual, part-time) workforces. Such organizational flexibility is supported by a shared culture of entrepreneurialism and fast decision-making. Murray (1989, p. 47) summarizes the new culture of post-Fordist capitalism:

Consumption has a new place. As for production the key word is flexibility – of plant and machinery, as of products and labour. Emphasis shifts from scale to scope, and from cost to quality. Organisations are geared to respond to rather than regulate markets. They are seen as frameworks for learning as much as instruments of control. Their hierarchies are flatter and their structures more open. The guerilla force takes over from the standing army. All this has liberated the centre from the tyranny of the immediate. Its task shifts from planning to strategy, and to the promotion of the instruments of post-Fordist control – systems, software, corporate culture and cash.

Post-Fordism is well suited to the growth of a 'service economy'. Since 1972 there has been a rapid decline in manufacturing matched by an accelerating growth of service employment that has taken place more in production and financial services as well as in sectors such as health and education, rather than in retailing, distribution or personal services (see Walker, 1985). Harvey (1989), while acknowledging the debate that surrounds analysis of this changing occupational structure, shows how the shift towards the production of services, especially of 'events', rather than the production of goods radically reduces the turnover time of consumption and thus accelerates accumulation.

The post-Fordist, flexibly accumulating, service economy is underpinned by the growth of an extraordinary system of international finance that is increasingly indifferent to the constraints of time or space. Computerized telecommunications allow instantaneous flows of money across the global market for finance and credit which disregards the boundaries of nation states and the temporalities of 'futures'. This trend illustrates a broader shift towards the contracting 'time–space distanciation' (Giddens, 1981, 1990) within the global village or, as Harvey (1989) conceptualizes it, the growing 'compression of our temporal and spacial worlds'.

The transformation of the environment provides a further illustration of the increasingly porous boundaries of the world we live in and have to share. Bhopal or Chernobyl have consequences that dissolve the distances of formal geography. Concern about the increasing degradation of the environment, and the multiple levels on which it is operating, grew during the 1980s. Locally, the mounting litter and traffic congestion disturb the quality of life, but the experience of acid rain is a regional phenomenon, while globally the accelerating emission of carbon dioxide and other 'greenhouse gases' into the atmosphere is great enough to cause a possible warming of the globe and, some claim, a melting of the ice caps. Added to the plunder of the rain forests, the steady erosion of topsoil, the destruction of countless rare species and damage to the ozone layer, these changes provide a catalogue of at least grave ecological concern and possibly disaster, if not for this generation then for the future. The consequences for a collective and shared environment of fragmented individual or group decisions, for example to produce or to use aerosols or refrigerators containing CFCs, are not always understood and raise issues about society and politics that we shall have to address in making sense of the changing nature of the public domain.

The cyclical and structural changes in the economy and the environment stand in complex relationship to equally fundamental changes in society. The flexible and service-oriented economy has had a transforming effect upon occupational and social structures. There has been a considerable expansion of the salariat and 'service class' occupations and a corresponding decline in semi-skilled and unskilled working class occupations. Marshall *et al.* (1988) acknowledge that there has been extensive upward mobility: 'perhaps as many as one-third of those presently in service class positions have arrived there from working class occupations' (p. 271). The differentiation of economic sectors and geographic locations together with the increasing segmentation of labour markets is creating greater heterogeneity and diversity of social groupings than traditional class ascriptions allow. For some (Bell, 1974, 1979), class structures themselves have given way to more fluidly graded socio-economic hierarchies. Andre Gorz (1982) has wished 'farewell to the working class'. The affluent worker, as Goldthorpe (1978) pointed out, had developed an instrumental attachment to work and collective commitments at work based upon sectional self-interest. When groups of workers organize together they do so as a means to individual ends rather than to meet the needs of their group, community or class as a whole.

Such a calculative orientation to occupational activity for many also reflects what Offe (1985) has called the 'decentring' of work within the lives of individuals. Family, the home and leisure pursuits more often preoccupy individuals, shape their identities and provide their lives with more meaning than their occupations and careers, which move to the periphery of their interests. Consumption rather than production affords the focus to people's lives. For Hobsbawm (1981), 'the values of consumer-society individualism and the search for private and personal satisfactions' have come to dominate society. This may be a rational response for the many who feel they have little sense of control over their destinies in the face of a public world that is in their perception growing more intractable.

> In so far as people have any sense of control over their own destinies this is more likely to be experienced in the private than in the public domain. The private domain may therefore be as crucial for the formation of social identities as the more public milieux of work and community. These social identities will play a crucial role in any analysis of the relationship between social structure and social action. Structural locations create arrays of potential interests, but interests depend upon people's perceptions of their social identity for their realisation in action.
>
> (Marshall *et al.*, 1988, p. 8)

The assumption that social identities are formed at work is misplaced as they are now more typically formed in the private domain. A more plural society is expressed in increasingly differentiated life-styles – of patterns of eating and dressing, of interests in music and the arts, of beliefs, religions and manners – which are held and lived out by diverse age groups, religious and ethnic minorities, by men and women in different family patterns. This reflects the more general emergence of the 'post-modern world' with its preference for difference over uniformity, fragmentation over integration, play and the ephemeral over purpose and form, and embraces the deep chaos of contemporary existence.

Increasingly privatized and individualized life-styles reflect the dominance of the consumer society, where choice appears an expression of freedom. The question 'who am I?' replaces the preoccupation of an earlier age, 'who are we?' As Bauman (1988) says, in the market society individuals have the opportunity, indeed the necessity, of self-assertion and self-construction though they are denied their need for self-confirmation. The competition and rivalry for distinction in shifting fashion and taste is a process of uncertainty. Lukes (1984) has argued that these changes reflect the disintegration of traditional moral frameworks in the face of the mechanisms of market seduction:

> There appears to have been a reactive growth (encouraged by a combination of recession and inflation) of inflation, pecuniary, egoistic, in short capitalistic values and attitudes, and

a disintegration of various moral frameworks within which these had a subordinate place and faced various countervailing forms of commitment, loyalty and discipline – whether based on unionism, locality or class.

With the unravelling of a moral order that established a framework of social responsibilities, individuals and groups pursue their interests to exploit their market situation. In the face of the seemingly intractable social and economic problems confronting society, individuals quietly retreat from the public domain into the satisfactions of the private sphere.

These changes in the social and class structure have created a more differentiated society. Yet research equally shows that there is no evidence for the disappearance or decomposition of class in British society. Studies at both Oxford and Essex show that despite increased complexity and mobility Britain remains a class society, with the service class more advantaged and exploiting opportunities more than the working class. Deeper structures of disadvantage and discrimination based on gender, race and class continue and deepen. The economic growth of the mid-1980s produced opulence for some in the face of continuing anxiety and alienation for those excluded (see Hudson and Williams, 1989):

> The elements and tendencies of a new polarisation can be assembled all too easily. . . . The rich have become richer and the poor poorer in Britain since 1979. . . . The stakes of individual success or failure in school or work are rising. Yet the odds of success or failure are lengthening along the lines of social division – between the inner city and the prosperous suburb, between the North and South, the white majority and the ethnic minorities, the privately and publicly schooled. In short, not a simple division into two nations, but a complex polarisation of increasingly embittered inequalities.
>
> (Halsey, 1986, p. 176)

The transformations of economy and society since the mid-1970s have generated a more political world as conceptions about ways of resolving the emerging problems have sharpened and fractured the post-war political consensus. A more assertive politics has developed at national and local levels as parties have sought to create distinctive ideologies and images in the eye of the electorate. Yet within the major parties new political perspectives have competed for dominance alongside the more traditional manifestos. The campaigning politics of 'the new right' and 'the new left' press for political change, arguing that the rhetorics of the past have failed. Meanwhile, a more strident politics of the centre has emerged to fill the vacuum created by the exit of the main conservative and socialist parties. Added to the politics of party are the new politics of movements: of parents in education, of the elderly ('grey power'), of consumers and, most significantly, the green movement campaigning for the protection of the environment.

Electoral politics have become more volatile as the electorate has appeared more willing to shift its allegiances, leading to more frequent changes of political control – at least at local level. During the 1980s the Alliance grouping often caused shifts in the balance of power locally, while some authorities became 'hung' as no party achieved an overall majority.

For some analysts, this volatility reflected the changing styles of social consumption described above. Dunleavy (1980) and others have argued that the electorate is fragmented along 'sectoral consumption cleavages'. How people consume housing or transportation or education influences their political allegiances. Consumption location rather than class determines how people will vote. For Crewe (1986), as well as Butler and Kavanagh (1984), these changes illustrate the weakening of the influence of class upon politics. 'Class dealignment', linked to a general loosening of the class structure, explains the electoral difficulties of the Labour Party at national level. Labour, by remaining a class party, has failed to appeal to the growing numbers of white collar workers. Countervailing arguments have been produced by Heath (1987) and Marshall *et al.* (1988), proposing that relative class voting has remained more or less constant. Labour's failures have political rather than social structural origins. Labour has performed poorly across its entire electoral base and not simply among the working class. But their evidence suggests that the political cohesiveness, or class identity, of the working class remains: 'Class interests are seemingly still central to the political process. There has been no transition to a post-industrial society in which the structure of class inequalities, together with class based political action, have given way to the purely status politics of the open society' (Marshall *et al.*, 1988, p. 274).

RE-EXAMINING THE POST-WAR ORDER

Such multiple changes indicate a society experiencing a phase of deep transition. The very language now being created to characterize this transformation – 'post-modern' (Heller and Fehrer, 1988; Harvey, 1989), 'post-industrial' (Bell, 1974), 'post-Fordist' (Hall and Jacques, 1989) – anticipates this historic juncture taking place. O'Connor (1973) speaks of a 'fiscal crisis' and Offe (1984) of a 'steering crisis', while Habermas (1976) points to a 'legitimation crisis'. Such structural change and uncertainty has provoked questions that further disturb the social and political cohesion of the post-war order.

Economic change, by making some members of society 'surplus to capacity', brings into question one of the bases of post-war citizenship – the right to work. The issues raised are quite fundamental. What will be the nature of work in the future and who will be required to work? Do individuals need to work to express their identities, develop their capacities, acquire status and contribute as citizens to the commonwealth of the community in which they live? Will those who remain outside work be regarded as 'members', as 'citizens', by others in the community? Will they be accorded equal rights, status and power in the community?

The trends towards differentiation that characterize post-modern society create space for innovation and change yet also threaten to undermine the very possibility of 'society'. Social fragmentation threatens the cooperation and trust that define a community and create the possibility of collective action, without which any society cannot survive (Gambetta, 1988). The most serious 'collective action problem' is the predatory exploitation of the environment, with its dramatic consequences for the quality of life and even its survival, as identified above. Mounting litter, traffic congestion and the prospect of global warming reveal the unintended collective consequences of our individual choices: self-interest can be self-defeating. The seductive yet ultimately irrational compulsion of some to 'free-ride' presents perhaps the most significant challenge for future society. Parfit (1984) succinctly describes the dilemma: 'it can be better for each if he adds to pollution, uses more energy, jumps queues and breaks agreements; but if all do these things that can be worse for each than if none do. It is very often true, that if each rather than none does what will be better for himself, this will be worse for everyone'. The question arises as to whether our society any longer possesses the social conditions to resolve the collective action problems that face it.

Underlying the quality of social cohesion are political issues. The fragmenting society is reflected in the fracture of the post-war consensus as agreement about membership, rights and distributive justice collapsed in the face of the uneven experience of change. Underlying the fiscal crisis (which led to a contraction of public expenditure: Gough, 1979; Hood and Wright, 1981) was actually a political crisis, as the willingness of many tax-payers to support the welfare of others crumbled (cf. Mishra, 1984). Has our society the political resources to respond to the social differentiation to which economic restructuring is a contributory cause? Anthony Crosland once claimed that no modern society has redistributed wealth without economic growth: yet coping with the present transition as much as that following the Second World War arguably requires agreement about the principles of distributive justice. Do the conditions exist to establish such a political settlement that underwrites everything else in society (Hirsch, 1977; Ellis and Kumar, 1983; Bauman, 1988; Dahrendorf, 1988)? The polity came to experience a crisis of legitimacy.

Social, economic and political changes have therefore, through the uncertainty they have generated, raised the most fundamental questions about what it is for a person to live or for a society to cohere during a period of transition:

* What is it to be a person? Is a person a passive being or possessed of powers and capacities that define his or her essential agency? As Taylor (1989) asks, what are 'the sources of the self'? What are the educational and social conditions for agency?
* Is there any such thing as society and what is it? Is a society no more than an aggregation of individuals or does it imply forms of social and linguistic community? What role does education play in preparing individuals for membership of society?
* What should be the nature of the polity? What is it to be a member of the polity? What rights and duties does membership imply? What distribution of power and wealth is consistent with justice and freedom? Who should take decisions and how? What forms of accountability and representation define our democracy? What role does education play in preparation for citizenship?

The effect of these structural changes and the questions they have given rise to has been to cause a fundamental re-examination of the post-war settlement and the social democratic polity it underwrote. The unremitting schedule of reforms to education and government since the mid-1970s has been in response to these crises. The state has been striving to establish the basis of a new social and political order that will meet the exigencies of a society experiencing a historic transformation. The restructuring entails conceptions about what it is to be a person, what form society and education should take, and what constitute legitimate rights and duties within the polity.

Two ostensibly alternative strategies for restructuring education and the post-war polity – corporatism and market consumerism – have been developed since the mid-1970s in response to the crisis. The next two chapters will consider each of these developments.

Chapter 4

The Period of Corporatism

The initial response of the British state to the crisis of the 1970s was to move from supporting to directing economy and society. Pahl (1977) and Winkler (1977) have conceptualized the processes of concentration and rationalization as leading to the creation of a *corporate state*. Corporatism seeks to impose four principles upon economy and society: *unity*, through the collaboration and cooperation of capital and labour; *order*, to achieve stability and discipline in industrial relations; *nationalism*, to reinforce indigenous interests; and *pragmatism* of ends and purposes, to ensure efficiency. Production replaces consumption as the important preoccupation of the state, while efficiency becomes the overriding priority, above the previous social democratic goals of equality and social justice. Pragmatism and efficiency are best facilitated by technocratic rational planning within more disciplined, bureaucratic organizational forms. The control and direction of education, because of its perceived function in preparing young people for their future roles in employment and society, becomes a central concern for the corporatist state.

By the mid-1970s education occupied a changed world and the responses to its multiple problems exemplify the modes of the corporate state. The corporatist agenda for restructuring education sought to adapt the service to the economic needs of the nation, to rationalize resources in order to improve efficiency and to establish a more unified and integrated system of accountable governance that could be controlled by Whitehall. These strategies of vocationalism, centralization and rationalization will be discussed in turn. Together they add up to a programme that undermined the post-war commitment to equal educational opportunities for all and resurrected the spectre of tripartism, of preparing young people to meet the layered needs of a differentiated labour market.

THE NEW VOCATIONALISM

The challenge to education from industry and society began to focus upon the transition from school to work. Many industrialists argued that schools were too self-absorbed and preoccupied with the social development of young people rather than preparing them for their economic roles in industry and commerce. The challenges coincided with the internal analyses by officials and HMI at the Department of Education and Science. Their internal memorandum, known as *The Yellow Book* (1976), argued that the weakness of secondary education was that it underprepared young people for employment: 'The time may now be ripe for change as the national mood and government policies have changed in the face of hard and irreducible facts.'

The call for a fundamental redirection of education required more political clout. It came from the Prime Minister. Callaghan's Ruskin speech launched a national debate, which was summarized in a Green Paper (1977). This concluded that schools were 'prejudiced against work in productive industry . . . that curricula are not related to the realities of most pupils' work after leaving school; and that pupils leave school with little or no understanding of the workings, or the importance, of the wealth producing sector of our economy'. The education service was answerable to society and should therefore contribute with other policy sectors 'to improving industrial performance and thereby increasing national wealth'. This government strategy to reorientate the education service was supported in Whitehall by the Treasury and the Cabinet Office: 'education has been isolated . . . and in future the output of schools will have to be keyed more tightly into employment needs' (DES, 1978).

Following a number of new appointments to senior positions in the DES, the Department itself became a driving force for education reconstruction, championing the initiative of strengthening the ties between school and work and between education and training, in order to improve the vocational preparation of the 14–19 age group. Restructuring would require complex changes to key components of the education system: schools would have to be rationalized, finance redirected and, critically, the curriculum and examinations would need to be recast. The DES believed that control of the curriculum was central to its purpose: 'our focus must be on the strategic questions of the content, shape and purpose of the education system and absolutely central to that is the curriculum'. Attention focused on the 16–19 sector because of its strategic location between secondary schooling and the world of work (or the prospect of unemployment) and because it was less hedged around by statutory constraints and so was more amenable to policy planning and change. The point was underlined by a senior official:

> the 16–19 area is one of the key means of changing the educational system and of achieving the relevance we desire because it sits at the watershed between school and work. If we can do things with the new 17 plus examination, that will give us an important lever to voca-tionalize or to re-vocationalize the last years of public schooling. That will be a very important, and significant, step indeed.

The reform of the 17 plus examination was one significant focus of strategy, seeking to give a vocational steer to the school curriculum. A case study of this strategic planning of change forms the subject of the next three sections.

Curriculum development for the 17 plus

To achieve its objective of introduction a vocational curriculum and examination at 17, the DES had first to negotiate intricate reforms in both the schools and the further education sector. While the problem in schools was said to be the inappropriateness of the traditional ('academic') offering, the problem in further education (FE) was defined as the need to rationalize a profusion of courses so tangled as to confound the investigator. Two DES committees (the Keohane and Mansell Committees) would be formed to clarify the 'client group', define their needs and review courses and modes of assessment.

In order to understand fully the work of those committees and the attempts to develop courses and exams at 17, a little of the historical context needs to be sketched. The initiative to develop the 17 plus began, in fact, in the 1960s; that is, during the period of the post-war education transformation. An understanding of the earlier development illuminates the contrast of educational purpose between the two periods, as well as the longevity of reform in education.

One of the first decisions of the newly created Schools Council in 1964 was to reappraise the post-16 curriculum in the light of the changing character of the sixth form and society in general. The excessive narrowness of advanced provision and the need to design courses for the 'new sixth' were immediate priorities. In 1968 the Council established a working party, led by Dr Briault (at that time the Education Officer for the Inner London Education Authority), to examine the curricular needs of young people who wished to remain at school or college for an extra year of general education. The working party's reports were published in 1972-3 as Working Papers 45/6.

The Briault Committee believed that the new sixth comprised a wide range of abilities and interests and, given the rapidity of social and economic change, the curriculum should be designed to reflect and encourage such diversity: 'schools and colleges will have to plan for diversity, allow for the later developer and the student who changes courses and make sure that no route is a dead end; we attach particular importance to this point – options must be kept open wherever possible'. The curriculum, it was proposed, should set a premium upon understanding, encouraging pupils to think and find connections across their studies. The new examinations should foster independence and originality of thought, allowing sufficient scope for the expression of personal qualities such as initiative, imagination and persistence in the carrying out of projects. The curriculum should, nevertheless, be balanced and relevant to the modern world, perhaps considering a vocational 'point of departure', although a common curriculum would be inappropriate to individual choice and need.

Briault proposed a Certificate of Extended Education (CEE) to be developed in a number of pilot schemes in association with the CSE exam boards. In 1976 the Council recommended that the experimental exam become formally recognized by the Secretary of State but neither Mr Mulley nor his successor, Mrs Williams, were prepared to give consent to CEE before decisions were made about the whole framework of 16–19 examinations and while employers were still expressing doubts about the usefulness of the new exam. In the autumn of 1977 the Secretary of State announced her intention to form the Keohane Committee to review CEE and its relationship to similar courses provided in FE colleges. The report of the Keohane Committee, *Proposals for a Certificate of Extended Education*, was published in December 1979. Early in 1978 the Mansell Committee was established by the Further Education Unit (FEU) at the DES to review the comparable non-advanced courses in colleges: their report, *A Basis for Choice* (ABC/7), was published in June 1979.

The two committees reviewing courses in the different education sectors came to many similar conclusions which distanced them from the aims and interpretations of the

Briault reports. Whereas the earlier review had described diversity of interests and abilities, both the Keohane and Mansell Committees believed the 'target groups' to comprise low-achieving young people of average ability who needed primarily 'to prepare themselves effectively for employment'. Both committees were in agreement about the aims of the curriculum, which should develop a vocational orientation that helped 'them understand what employers will expect from them [and] what they should expect from employment'; courses should 'encourage the development of a *realistic* vocational emphasis' (emphasis added). Both committees believed, therefore, that employers' needs and demands should acquire priority in curriculum design.

Although the two committees agreed that the courses should lead to employment and vocationally oriented certificates, their conception of the design of the courses and assessment reflected sectoral interests traditions and practices. Keohane proposed common proficiency tests in literacy and numeracy within courses that retained the traditional school principle of individually chosen single subjects culminating in an examination. Nevertheless, the Keohane committee conceded that the model for such pre-employment courses lay in the tradition of further education, where the distinctive grouped curriculum was designed as an integration of the elements the providers believed the students *should* acquire. The Mansell Committee report in June 1979 advocated criteria and a model that would articulate the distinctiveness of the non-advanced FE tradition while rationalizing the plethora of existing provision. The structure of their curriculum would comprise a well-defined common core of studies together with general vocational and job-specific studies (for example, experiencing the work of garage hand, typist or carpenter). A profile assessment system, rather than exams, would provide detailed records of experience and assess performance and attainment, as well as personal qualities. In short, Keohane's CEE proposed separate courses leading to exams, while Mansell's ABC proposed one course leading to profile assessment. School and college would develop vocational preparation courses to suit their own institutions and traditions.

While the Secretary of State deliberated on these two reports, the disparate interests voiced their competing claims. The Certificate of Secondary Education (CSE) Exam Boards, the Schools Council and the teacher unions urged their support for the findings of Keohane, while the FE institutes, the FEU and the National Association of Teachers in Further and Higher Education (NATFHE) proclaimed the virtues of the Mansell report. In October 1980 the Government finally set out its policy in a consultative paper, *Examinations 16-18*, which recommended in favour of the FEU report. The Green Paper concluded that 'members of the target group in both sectors can best be served by provision more akin to traditional FE developed in the light of *A Basis for Choice*'. Accordingly, the Government proposed that CEE be eliminated expeditiously because it was insufficiently vocationally oriented and left too much discretion to schools. The development of the pre-vocational courses would pass to one of the FE validating bodies (probably the City and Guilds of London Institute, CGLI); the General Certificate of Education (GCE) and CSE boards were to be excluded.

Such a firm prescriptive decision should, ostensibly, have eliminated equivocation and established the authority of the Department amid rival contending interests. But the schools sector – for example, the CSE Boards, the Schools Council, the National Union of Teachers (NUT) and the College Principals – led an immediate, vociferous and well-orchestrated challenge against the narrow definition of the student group and its needs, against what they believed to be the manifest steering of young people into vocational routes without opportunities for educational progression, and tacitly against arrangements that encroached arbitrarily upon their financial interests. Effective political support was mobilized for their demands within the DES, which was beginning to fracture according to the different interests of its internal branches. Ministers and officials were beginning to take sides in the confrontation between the education and training sectors. The organized resistance achieved two important concessions: first, only two months after publication of the Green Paper, it was announced that the CSE Boards were to be incorporated in the validation of the new exam; and second, when the Government finally published the details of the new 17 plus exam in May 1982 the contents had been redrafted to accommodate schools' interests. The curriculum would remain vocationally oriented, retain work experience and continue to prepare young people effectively for employment. But the course was now aimed at students 'with a wide range of interests, expectations and abilities', who needed a 'broad programme of general education' that would prepare them for 'adult life' as well as for work. The curriculum would offer a core of basic studies before elective options were chosen in technical, business and general studies: development work in the latter would need to build upon the pioneering work of the CSE and GCE exam boards. A certificate of pre-vocational education (CPVE) would be accorded to all students, recording details of performance, although attainment of key aspects – maths, English and science – would have to be externally assessed or moderated. A consortium of interested parties – CGLI, CSE and GCE, the Royal Society of Arts and the Technical and Business Education Councils (TBEC) – would administer the new exam under a chairman appointed by the Secretary of State.

The CPVE did not resolve the underlying conflict between sectoral interests and it was not long before an effective counter-revolt was mounted by the world of further education. The FEU was concerned about the continuing stress upon 'subjects', together with the implicit persistence of exams. However, the CGLI refused to take part in the consortium and resolved to prolong the experiment with its own 17 plus vocational course, which it had introduced unilaterally in the previous autumn. The BEC also made it clear that it was not prepared to lose to the consortium fee income from 17 plus courses that it already controlled and validated. The end of 1982 was to see the reassertion of FE dominance of the 17 plus. Control of the initiative shifted within the DES from Schools Branch to Higher and Further Education Branch, which was soon proclaiming a new initiative from CGLI, TEC and BEC to provide a joint FE body to run the new exam. The idea of a consortium was dropped and courses run by other interests were to be accredited by the joint body.

Conceptualizing the codes of curriculum change

The central trust of the curriculum development inherent in these proposals was to negotiate for schools and colleges a vocational curriculum that would prepare the great majority of so-called 'non-advanced' students for their economic roles in industry and commerce. Priorities and values had shifted: training was preferred to education, practical skills were elevated above understanding, detailed profiles replaced impersonal exams and external control of the curriculum by employers and administrators displaced the influence of the professional community of teachers. How can such changes in the

16–19 curriculum be understood and what analytical concepts allow us to interpret their meaning?

In its structuring of selected knowledge and experience the curriculum operates to produce and reproduce a system of values and power in society (Williams, 1961; Bernstein, 1975; Lawton, 1980). This relationship has been developed imaginatively in the work of Bernstein and provides an appropriate means of gaining conceptual purchase upon the changes to the 17 plus curriculum described above. Bernstein proposes that the educational experience of young people is shaped by curricula, which define what is to count as valid knowledge, and pedagogic processes, which determine acceptable forms for the transmission of knowledge. Underlying and unifying the message systems of curriculum and pedagogy are principles or codes that regulate the structure of knowledge (classification) and the processes of transmission (framing). Classification, referring to the extent of differentiation and insulation of curricula contents, seeks to focus attention upon the forms of power that maintain and reproduce the boundaries between categories. Framing, on the other hand, refers to the context in which knowledge is transmitted and, by defining the principles that regulate what may be transmitted, seeks to conceptualize the underlying principles of control. The strength of classification and framing and their relationship to each other reveal the underlying codes of meaning and power: power and control are made substantive in the classification and framing procedures that shape educational contexts and practices.

Bernstein's typology of educational codes – 'collection' and 'integrated' – and the shift he discerns taking place between dominant codes, reflects and illuminates the changes to the 17 plus curriculum in the early 1980s. I shall discuss collection and integrated codes in turn. Collection codes typify the secondary school curriculum, with its purest expression at advanced level GCE yet equally reflected in the proposals for a Certificate of Extended Education. The proposals here reinforced the value of specialized knowledge through compartmentalized subjects. The purity of specialized knowledge is protected not only through the maintenance of subject boundaries but also through the ordering of pupils who, streamed and graded, must demonstrate capacity by passing through ritual exams to attain selected membership of more advanced stages. The Keohane allegiance to single examinable subjects sought to reproduce this curricular format in the CEE, and also, therefore, traditional modes of framing. Framing is typically weaker in English education than in many European countries and this allows a greater variety of teaching styles. Nevertheless, such weak framing grants essential control to teachers, who can, didactically, regulate selection and transmission of educational knowledge.

It is an important characteristic of framing under collection codes that what is being regulated is the pupils' access to realms of knowledge that are detached from the immediacy of everyday life: the universal replaces the particular, the abstract and distant replaces the familiar and common sense. Yet the strength of this framing has often varied with the 'ability' of the pupils, so that the less advanced slower-learning students are exposed to learning situations much less removed from day-to-day experience. This weak framing, reflected in the construction of the Keohane CEE, is often associated, Bernstein alludes, 'with purpose of social control'.

The dominant modes of control underlying collection codes rest upon principles of academic hierarchy and surveillance, upon selective and ritualized socialization and, most significantly, upon the maintenance of strong boundaries that insulate packages of knowledge in ways that render them predictable and controllable: 'knowledge and the principles of social order are made safe if knowledge is subdivided, well insulated and transmitted by authorities who themselves view their own knowledge or disciplines with the jealous eye of a threatened priesthood'. A divided curriculum is a controlled curriculum. Yet differentiated curricula typically create differentiated individuals with varying experiences and specific identities. Because the focus is upon the ordering of knowledge rather than upon persons (or at least only upon persons indirectly) the spaces within and between boundaries allow individuals privacy, thus reducing 'the penetration of the socialisation process, for it is possible to distance oneself from it'.

The invasion of personal privacy is, however, one of the distinctive consequences of a shift in education from collection to integrated codes. Bernstein perceives such a movement taking place in English education, as yet unrealized and incomplete, but exemplified, he argues, in the typical 'Plowden-inspired' primary school and in curriculum developments like the Nuffield science project. Bernstein is, therefore, describing and conceptualizing changes that were emerging during the first post-war transformation of education. Yet the shift to an integrated curriculum is more than ever manifest in the proposals – during the second phase transformation – for a pre-vocational course and assessment at 17. The paradox of continuity and contrast in coding between the two periods will require analysis below.

An integrated curriculum, as described by Bernstein, is characterized by an openness that 'blurs the boundaries between subjects'. The integrated curriculum shifts the emphasis from knowledge as isolated compartments to the notion of curriculum contents standing in a necessary interrelationship and thus needing to be open to each other. The integrated curriculum also sees a shift in framing from the idea of 'bodies' of knowledge being imparted to passive students, to 'ways of knowing' and thus to students' self-discovery of knowledge. The focus is upon the student and his or her learning needs and difficulties. The shift to an integrated code embodies the values and assumptions of the first education transformations from the late 1950s. The task then was to develop, in the educational interests of young people, a more sophisticated understanding of what should count as valid knowledge, together with appropriate conceptions of teaching and learning. Under collection codes it had only been the academic élite who, socialized through successive levels of bounded knowledge, were admitted finally to the realization that knowledge itself was provisional and socially constructed rather than an objective product. Integrated codes, however, *begin* the teaching process with this understanding, seeking to encourage *all* young people to explore more openly the principles of knowledge creation. The Schools Council's CEE, although it had its roots in the tradition of collection codes, sought to develop experimentally along the path towards integration. Thus *even* low-achieving students were to be encouraged to explore connections between their studies and to use project material to think imaginatively and independently about the creation of and principles underlying new knowledge.

Changes in teaching style would accompany such experiments in unifying and elaborating CEE curricula. The weaker framing of integrated codes reduces the control of teachers as didactic styles give way to cooperative styles: 'from schools which emphasised the teacher as solution giver to schools which emphasise the teacher as problem-poser or creator . . . in a context of self-discovery by pupils: the act of learning itself celebrates choice' (Bernstein, 1975, p. 70). This teaching style, Bernstein believed, would generate a marked trend towards a common system of transmitting and evaluating educational knowledge: 'in other words integrated codes will, at the level of teachers, probably create homogeneity in teaching practice'. The proposals for a CEE envisaged teachers organizing together to achieve consensus about purpose, themes and styles and perhaps teaching together in teams where appropriate.

Such principles of teaching practice suggest the dominant modes of control underlying integrated codes. Whereas collection codes rest upon strength of boundary and thus the control of access to knowledge, integrated codes depend upon collectivity and consensus, and this control is based upon persons and relationships. The opening of the boundaries of knowledge to explore the various principles that underpin its creation and re-creation requires and stimulates the opening of organizational boundaries as teachers and pupils are required increasingly to extend relationships across hierarchical and disciplinary divisions. Altered conceptions of knowledge, of its transmission, may well, Bernstein suggests, 'bring about a disturbance in the structure and distribution of power'. Horizontal organizational controls replace vertical deference. Committees of teachers across the curriculum are likely to convene and make explicit underlying themes and principles, the collective roles that should be developed and the means of socializing teachers and pupils into the chosen educational code. The code presupposes a 'high level of ideological consensus', and without such agreement and shared commitment the system is likely to founder.

It was the openness of the integrated code that arguably represented such an educational advance in the Briault CEE, as in other curriculum developments during the first educational transformation. Yet Bernstein expresses forebodings about integrated codes and their potential for intensified social controls upon young people. Open frames increase the potential influence and participation of students in the learning process, but equally areas of privacy become eroded as more of the students' capacities and attributes are given to learning:

> the weak frames enable a greater range of the students' behaviour to be made public, and they make possible considerable diversity (at least in principle) between students. It is possible that this might lead to a situation where assessment takes more into account 'inner' attributes of the student. Thus if he has the 'right' attitudes, then this will result later in the attainment of various specific competences. The 'right' attitude may be assessed in terms of the fit between the pupils' attitudes and the current ideology. It is possible then, that the evaluative criteria of integrated codes with weak frames as these refer to specific cognitive attributes but strong as these refer to dispositional attributes. If this is so then a new range of pupil attributes become candidates for labels. It is also likely that the weakened classification and framing will encourage more of the pupil student to be made public, more of his thoughts feelings and values. In this way more of the student is available for control. As a result the socialisation process could be more intensive and perhaps more penetrating.
> (Bernstein, 1975, p. 109)

Openness is Janus-headed: depending upon the context, openness can be designed to facilitate the learning process of the student or her control and subordination.

It is the argument here that the forebodings of Bernstein about the emerging integrated code of the late 1960s were in fact being realized in the developing integrated codes of corporatism, as illustrated in particular in the Keohane or Mansell proposals for a vocational certificate at 17. There were common elements between the codings of the periods of social democracy and corporatism. The overriding theme of vocationalism provides the relational idea, which subordinates the distinctiveness of separate subjects and erodes the boundaries that protect their independence. Weak framing could be said to accompany weak classification. Pedagogic style requires consensus among teachers about underlying themes and principles, while the more open frames extend the range of qualities and attributes students are expected to bring to the learning process.

The differences in the integrated codes between the different periods of educational change are striking, however. Classification under vocational coding in fact remains particularly strong, erecting a firm boundary between knowledge and practice and supported by consensual definitions of acceptable transmission. Now for an increasing proportion of young people the practical, the familiar and immediate, common sense and everyday knowledge, become the subject of the curriculum, displacing the analytical and cognitive, the unusual and distant, the universal. By constructing a firm boundary between mental and manual knowledge the mode of control implicit in collection codes, of insulation diffusing dangerous knowledge, is retained and reinforced in the coding of vocational curricula. In fact the framing of such curricula is as strong under collection codes because there is no shift in power, as anticipated, from teachers to students. Rather than working out from the needs of individual young people the teaching process continues to be based on the transmission of an equally rigid framework of learning. Moreover, the close monitoring of character and performance through detailed profiling becomes not an unintended consequence, but the explicit purpose of evaluation and certification.

Thus although integrated codes of the corporatist period involve a change, for an increasing number, in what is to count as having knowledge, there is no such change as Bernstein suggested in the structure and distribution of power: in fact there is an intensification of the existing power structure, which is operating to tighten the bonds of socialization and control. As Bernstein could hardly have anticipated, the integrated codes of vocationalism are reintroducing the 'deep closure of [Durkheim's] mechanical solidarity': a homogeneous world of low individuation in which people are assigned to their social roles and held together by common ties and rigid codes of conduct and sentiment. How are we to account for such developments?

Explaining the restructuring of the 17 plus curriculum

I have described the protracted development, competitively negotiated between the schools and further education sectors, of a vocational curriculum at 17. Bernstein's 1975 book has provided the means of conceptually mapping these changes, but not of explaining them. How are we to account for the development and assertion of the new vocational code, with its distinctive implications for educational socialization and control? I shall examine two frameworks that are particularly appropriate to an account of the struggles to implement a new curriculum at 17. The first constructs an explanation around the interests and power of the key actors in a social network, while the second identifies the structural problems and dilemmas of the social system as the central explanatory axis.

The first theory is based on concepts of interest exchange and power (see Archer, 1979, 1981; Rhodes, 1981, 1988). The theory conceives the relations between levels of government as forming a complex network of organizations, agencies and interest groups. These 'actors' live in an environment of uncertainty produced by the scarcity of resources necessary to ensure survival. They can pursue their interests and acquire the strategic resources necessary for managing uncertainty only by escaping or creating dependencies among the other actors. Autonomy and power provide the critical bargaining levers to manipulate exchange relationships in the network. The operation of the network is shaped by the pattern of resource ownership and the structure of dependencies. Resources are defined broadly, for example as finance or authority or information. To monopolize the ownership of such critical resources is to create dependencies, exact compliance and accrue power. Blau (1964) sought to articulate the conditions that actors must meet if they are to maximize autonomy and bargaining power in an exchange relationship: first, possess strategic resources that others may desire; second, ensure that these resources are scarce and unavailable elsewhere; third, have the capacity to use coercive sanctions if necessary; fourth, be indifferent to the resources possessed by other actors.

Governments since the mid-1970s have defined the 17 plus as critical to their plans to introduce a more vocationalized curriculum for the 14–19 age group, but lacking the instruments of control possessed by more centralized systems they have had to rely on exchange and to deploy what resources they have had accordingly. Actors within the DES favoured the language and imagery of bargaining:

> We operate within the structure of a persuasion game; we have to move people a long way from their initial position and this requires numerous steps and strategems.

> Mostly my role has been one of honest broker to bring the warring factions together; I use HMI a lot who are very good at carpet bagging between different interests through informal and formal meetings.

> We are very much in the brokerage game, fixing and dealing with powerful independent bodies with deep traditions and independent sources of wealth and property; exchanges were inevitably going to be protracted.

In this context the DES sought to deploy its strategic resources to achieve maximum leverage in bargaining. Control of financial resources was gradually being concentrated at the centre to reduce the discretion of the schools sector, while the limited grants available to the independent bodies, boards and institutes had been manipulated to provide appropriate curricular developments. Monopoly power over the rules of the game had been used to shape circulars and official papers as well as to refuse legal recognition to the CEE. Not only had official committees and their composition been determined and their agendas defined, but where possible constitutional rights had been activated to facilitate appointments – 'this is one of our main influences and controls: where we can appoint a chairman and his council we take the opportunity where necessary'. Controls over finance and the rules of the game changed the structure of exchange and the possibility of reciprocation. Coercive sanctions had been applied to undermine the Schools Council or to exclude the CSE exam boards, or to manoeuvre control within the DES branches to limit access and influence to sources of political power. Perhaps the centre's most subtle and pervasive resource was the capacity to articulate and promote new educational ideologies, to lend authority to new integrated codes that underwrote the message systems of curricula, pedagogy and evaluation. The new belief systems shaped the pattern of indifference to opposition resources, as well as the rates of exchange for these resources.

The schools resisted the encroachment upon their territory implied by the state's support for a vocational oriented exam at 17. Alliances were mobilized within the DES and

among ministers to ensure that bargaining over the 17 plus proposals reflected concessions to the sometimes traditional collection code interests of schools and teachers. A
few sanctions may have been displayed to reinforce the assertion of their position. But
although compromises were achieved, the bargaining position of the schools sector had
been particularly weak and vulnerable: the resources available had been limited and they
lacked support at the centre of government, where new ideologies rendered the powerful
indifferent to the skills and resources that schools had to offer. Dependence upon external resources and commitment to skills and values that lacked general currency undermined the interests and influence of the schools sector.

The strategies and transactions of the disparate further education sector actors are
also illuminated by this explanatory framework. Their monopoly of vocational expertise, and domination of FE income derived from those markets, supported the interests
of the world of further education in the development of a (integrated code) vocationally
orientated certificate of employability. Institutes such as the CGLI used their considerable legal and financial autonomy to seize the initiative during periods of inertia and
thus to increase their subsequent bargaining power. The educational ideologies of
integrated curricula articulated by FE colleges, associations and institutes reflected the
purposes of those at the centre of power and made the state more sensitive to the
demands and potential use of sanctions by FE interests.

Here appears to be a plausible framework that does much to help us explain complex
developments in the 17 plus curriculum. The model suggests that the actors who monopolized resources expanded their own autonomy and achieved the compliance of others.
Yet there were actors within both the schools and FE who possessed wealth and autonomy without acquiring concomitant influence. The stress within the model upon
resources does not fully account for the unfolding of the story. In particular, those
organizations which had enjoyed closer institutional ties with the state, for example the
FEU or the validating bodies TEC and BEC, grew in influence and impact over their
rivals *within* FE as well as in the school sector. There are a number of deficiencies in
this model, however, which render its assumptions problematic. First, there is an
assumption about the nature of the actors which derives from the cultural source of the
model: American studies of coordination problems among competing welfare agencies.
In this case the organizations were relatively equal. Such assumptions are inappropriate
when the focus becomes the relationship between the state and other organizations: the
relationship is different in kind. Second, the argument from resource primacy seems
tenable as long as the definition is drawn widely, but greater conceptual specificity
leaves the proposition vulnerable empirically. Third, a different understanding of actors
and resources would undermine the assumption of exchange, which presupposes that
all actors can renegotiate their position with a little shrewd 'politicking'. But some transactions are likely to be unequal intrinsically: the state in the last resort will be able to
find the powers and resources to win most encounters.

The explanatory power of the resource dependency theory diminishes in effect
when one of the actors ineluctably has recourse to monopoly powers to change the
rules of the game, to eliminate summarily inconvenient competitors while creating
others in its own image, to control resources but also to manipulate the currency
and the rate of exchange, and to possess in reserve an array of sanctions. The state is
not one actor among others but dominates the contemporary stage. To grasp fully the
state-led restructuring of education at the present time we need to theorize exchange

transactions within a broader understanding of social structure and its contextual problems.

STEERING CAPACITY AND CENTRALIZATION

The corporate purposes of vocationalism and restructuring education presupposed appropriate organizational means. With the deepening crises of the 1970s the state became increasingly preoccupied with re-examining relationships within the political system in order to clarify and redefine control. Habermas (1976) argued that the deepening economic crises of the 1970s created 'steering problems' for the state. To maintain control and integration the state had to respond by progressively extending its boundaries, its tentacles of political leverage into the economic and social subsystems. The extension of steering capacity presupposed the emergence of new modes of rationality, or forms of technical knowledge about the working of society. These modes depended upon forms of power that relied less on the exercise of command and more on indirect forms of control – such as technically efficient rules and procedures. Offe (1975) took the argument further. The state, in order to maintain its functions of system integration, was increasingly driven to develop new forms of intervention. The minimalist role of central control of overall aggregate resources was increasingly inadequate, and the state was constrained to adopt a productive mode to sustain and develop the system's economic infrastructure, progressively intervening in 'education skills, technological change, control over raw materials, health, transportation, housing, the structure of cities, physical environment, energy and communication services'. This extension of steering capacity presupposed the emergence of new modes of rational planning and new knowledge about services and policies. The new mode of intervention called for 'stricter controls of objectives, outputs and outcomes by such techniques as program budgeting, cost-benefit analysis and social indicators' (Offe, 1975, pp. 141–2). To ensure system maintenance and the development of infrastructures the state was driven into progressively detailed planning and production of economic and public service activities.

Both Blau and Schoenherr (1971) and Offe (1975) were aware that what was crucial for an understanding of new state systems of policy planning was their form and mode rather than any particular content of policy. Here they did no more than extend Weber's (1968) formulation of contemporary rationality. Specifically modern rationality, he argued, denoted not only means–end instrumentality but, more importantly, the pervasive application of formally abstract procedures based upon increasingly specialized and technical concepts. The convergence of purposive and formal rationality ensured maximum precision, calculability and control of decision processes. Implicit in the rules were the ends to be pursued and the interests served. Offe was particularly articulate on the matter:

> the formal rules that give structure and continuity to the operation of the state apparatus are not merely instrumental procedures designed to carry out or implement political goals or to solve social problems. They do determine themselves, in a hidden and unexplicit way, what potential goals are and what problems have the chance to come up on the agenda of the political system. Thus it is not only true *that* the emergence of a social problem puts into motion the procedural dynamics of policy formation, program design and implementation but, also, conversely, the institutionalized formal mode of operation of political

institutions determines what potential issues are, how they are defined, what solutions are proposed, and so on.

(Offe, 1975)

Confronted by problems of control and integration, the state develops new policy planning processes as modes of rationality that are particularly appropriate to system strains and contradictions. The education subsystem appeared to conform to such an analysis.

Policy planning from the Department of Education and Science

Given a firm Department view about the conception and direction that education should take in a period of change, the hidden ambiguities of the DES's role were revealed: responsible for change but unable to secure policy implementation for its conception of change. A DES initiative presupposed greater control from the centre than existed, a capacity to lead, intervene and shape change that it did not have. Although the 1944 Education Act had divided powers systematically between partners to the service, the local authorities had strengthened their influence and control during the 1960s. Thus the DES would need to arrest the decline in its influence and reassert control over its partners.

The DES had been exhorted to develop rational centralized policy planning systems in a critical report produced by the OECD (1975). Reviewing the DES's policy planning processes in the early 1970s, 'the examiners' believed that the Department remained essentially incrementalist in its planning, merely seeking to effect improvements within existing structures or assumptions, which presuppose 'that the basic directions of educational development are largely foreclosed – determined one infers by historical circumstances, demographic trends and changes in public attitudes'.

The OECD examiners were critical about a planning system that was passive, reactive and static rather than dynamic and proactive. The Department should, they argued, be continually reviewing its goals, objectives and purposes in the light of changing knowledge and values rather than being merely preoccupied with its traditional concerns of scale, organization and resources: 'the stress laid on the "input" . . . severely constricts the role which planning for education could play in the general social development of the country' (OECD, 1975, p. 42). It was this lack of educational perspective that most concerned the examiners. There seemed to be no attempt by the DES to situate its policies and plans within a changing context and even more significantly no attempt to re-evaluate the context and purposes of education for a changing world:

> at no point does the White Paper bring the structure of the education function into perspective, either for the individual over the whole of his life span, or for innovation to meet economic, technical and social change. We miss a balanced analysis of persisting and new trends in society, in technological development and in the role of the state and of the place of education and science in the process of evolution.
>
> (OECD, 1975, p. 34)

In a world in which the knowledge, skills and values of the past were continually being brought into question, there seemed to be no attempt in the DES to identify and formulate new educational objectives for a changing world. At the centre of the Department's policy planning in the 1970s, the OECD argued, should have been the educational needs of the 16–19 age group. The DES retorted that this criticism was unfair because although the 16–19s were excluded from consideration in the 1972 White Paper, other needs were reserved by the Department for specific and subsequent consideration. Nevertheless, the examiners believed this omission to be particularly unfortunate and serious:

> it seems surprising that neither the rapid expansion of resource needs for education in the 1960s nor the specific problems of economic growth and social progress in the UK impelled the government or the other departments to develop an integrated or at least coordinated approach to this vital challenge to industrial society.
>
> (OECD, 1975, p. 36)

The OECD believed that the neglect of the needs of 16–19s in a changing society reflected the 'closed' planning procedures of the DES. The needs of young people were increasingly for vocational preparation. The examiners exhorted the DES to acknowledge the interdependence of education and training in terms of skills, knowledge and attitudes required to adapt to changing circumstances. The education service should increasingly view itself not as a separate institution but rather in terms of the functions it performs for society and economy.

The role of the DES in the late 1970s, in promoting vocational education and in rationalizing scarce resources, would have impressed its erstwhile examiners. The DES sought to develop the powers and controls that would enable it to restructure the education system according to redefined purposes, roles and authority relations in a period of rapid socio-economic change. Thus a senior DES official commented:

> We are seeking to restructure education. To do so we need control. There is a need especially in the 16–19 area for a centrally formulated approach to education: we need what the Germans call *Instrumentarium* through which Ministers can implement and operate policy. The DES has sought to steer a number of dimensions of policy – finance, institutional reorganization, staffing quality – but above all in curriculum and assessment. . . . I see a return to centralization of a different kind with the centre seeking to determine what goes on in institutions: this is a more fundamental centralization than we have seen before.

We need to explore how the Department came to terms with its inadequate array of powers and instruments in order to secure its policy objectives. The Department had to begin by drawing upon a variety of strategies and instruments to facilitate its policy: 'Education is such a complex, pluralist institution that to achieve one limited goal you have to make five or six interrelated moves: it's rather like playing a fugue using the device of theme and counterpoint' (a Secretary of State). The DES sought more direct hierarchical controls like those it envied in the MSC. The strategies deployed have embraced persuasion (promotion, co-option and advice), pressure and manipulation, and control (bureaucratization and regulation). Each will be discussed in turn, illustrated from the 16–19 area.

Persuasion

Since the late 1970s the Department had been very successful in promoting its 16–19 policies through a stream of speeches, statements in Parliament, Green Papers and circulars. The process of persuasion had also been pursued by co-opting professional and political representatives from local government on to working parties and policy review committees – thus the Expenditure Steering Group (Education) (ESGE) 16–19,

Sub-group on 16–19, and its successor, the Macfarlane Committee, were established to help build consensus about 16–19 policy:

> We wanted Macfarlane because we wanted to carry the LEAs with us politically as well as professionally. This engagement of the LEAs is critical. The problem with the LEAs is not one of local variation, it is rather the political problem of individual LEAs against the collectivity of LEAs and thus the problem of implementation. It is no good just talking to the Associations . . . thus our strategy of overall planning and orchestration. But some LEAs nevertheless always fall out.

We need to note that these working parties and committees were not commissions or the old Advisory Committees. Their existence, membership and agendas are firmly under the control of the Department. We should also note that they were committees of the providers of education; that is, the DES and the LEAs: 'those who have the power and the money, the local authorities and ourselves: the managers and the paymasters should sit down and get something done'. The teachers were excluded.

The Department sought further to persuade LEAs by preparing forms of practical advice about the methods and procedures of rationalization of institutions: 'our task is to confront LEAs with the severity of the situation and the need for rationalization . . . we must identify options for them, tell them how to approach the problem methodologically – by defining the client groups for them and the courses which should be provided: we aim to give practical advice to LEAs'.

Pressure

The Department, as well as deploying the arts of persuasion, had sought to bring more direct pressure upon local authorities by requesting and manipulating information and by introducing financial instruments that steered policy in the required directions. The DES requested LEAs to provide information about surplus places in schools and their policies for the curriculum. Asking local authorities for information about their policies and provision offered opportunities for the centre to steer the service: 'knowledge about the education service is a source of power and influence to the DES'.

Information could be used to exert an indirect, though potentially greater, influence upon local decision-making. Sections of the 1980 Education Act made it a duty for local authorities to publish information about each of their schools, including information 'as may be required by regulations made by the Secretary of State' on the performance of schools as indicated by their examination results. Such information would help parents to express a preference for a particular school. DES officials no less than ministers were in no doubt about the significance of such policies for the rationalization of institutions. A little healthy competition would constrain LEAs to reorganize and close unpopular schools: 'The 1980 Act gives powers to the centre to control information. It is an indirect power seeking to influence parents directly and LEAs indirectly. It is . . . a means of managing falling school rolls by letting popular (over-subscribed) schools expand and others wither away (become under-subscribed).'

The systematic reporting and publication of information would, it was hoped, influence and manipulate local authorities. When linked to other policy instruments information could provide more positive steering capacity. The Department believed that the mechanisms of grant support to local authorities could become major instruments of leverage over policy. For example, information about surplus capacity fed into the rate support grant negotiations could constrain local authorities to make savings and rationalize their provision. It was, however, through the new block grant system that the DES intended to bring the most influence to bear upon LEAs. The grant-related expenditure (GRE) mechanisms of the block grant would make the link between an authority's grant share and its actual expenditure a basis for influencing more directly its pattern of expenditure:

> This would involve a continuing dialogue with the authority on the broad thrust of its education policies, and it would doubtless be hard to prevent a similar dialogue with local interest groups and even individuals. DES ministers have not ruled out the possibility of exploiting the potential which may be inherent in the block grant system, for obtaining more information about and influence over the policies of individual LEAs. . . . This would bring about a major shift in DES–LEA relationships.

However, the DES failed to win its own education block grant and had not sought to use the GRE mechanisms in any extensive way to influence LEA policy. The mechanisms had, however, begun to be used. GREs had been

> calculated on the basis of surplus capacity being withdrawn. This is a very real issue. The expenditure White Paper plans to assume that closures have in fact taken place. The savings therefore have already been taken away and if the LEAs do not rationalize institutions they will have to make cuts elsewhere in their budgets.

Finance was also being used more positively to provide incentives for LEAs to follow the policy priorities of the centre. Some £60 million of additional resources were made available as a financial incentive to local authorities to encourage young people to stay on at school – to pursue courses of pre-vocational preparation. LEAs that increased their participation rates could expect to win more grants. Grants were made available to LEAs that had submitted acceptable proposals to develop a practical curriculum for less able 14–16-year-olds. This principle of financial incentives through specific grants had now been embodied in the 1984 Education Act (Grants and Awards). It reflected Departmental strategy: 'we in the DES are for targeting and indicative planning'.

Control

Persuasion, pressure and manipulation could strengthen but not secure central policy initiatives. The DES had sought to gain control by extending bureaucracy and by legislating extended powers of regulation over local authorities.

The Department attempted to introduce a greater sense of organizational structure and hierarchy into a disparate and diffuse educational system. LEAs were directed to report information to the centre; relations with local authority representatives became formalized through the ESGE; Her Majesty's Inspectors (HMI) were encouraged to play their part within a framework of directions established by the Department; territorial officers were requested to play a more assertive role in relation to LEAs. More significantly, in the field of the curriculum and examinations, the demise of the Schools Council was confirmed because of its independence (there was no means of 'coercing' the Secretary and there was a need for a more 'submissive staff', the DES claimed). The Council was replaced by separate curriculum and examination committees tied more closely to the Department. In the FE sector curriculum development was promulgated by the Further Education Unit, influenced and appointed by the DES.

More significant than these organizational developments was the increased capacity to regulate LEA practice. The Department used its ultimate powers of legislation (1980 and 1981 Education Acts) to extend its potential for direct control and regulation of LEAs. Sections 12–16 of the 1980 Act are important for the subject of this chapter. The need for most LEAs to reorganize their institutions and submit proposals to the Secretary of State brings the Department to centre stage in a crucial policy area. Sections 12–14 increase the capacity to intervene in LEA proposals despite Circular 2/80's restraining words – local proposals should not be modified so as to be changed in substance. However, as one official acknowledged, 'we could still do quite a lot'. The rejection and amendment of Manchester's proposal was undoubtedly a significant modification by the centre of a local initiative. Section 15 provided the centre with the mechanism to regulate the admission limits for each school over time. If a school roll fell 20 per cent below a published admission base line (for 1979) then the section 12 procedure was triggered: the LEA must then publish notices to such effect together with its response, which allows the Secretary of State the opportunity to call in the proposals for his or her approval or modification. Section 15 was therefore, in the words of a DES official, 'a major addition to the powers of the Secretary of State: in this case to regulate the reduction of school places'.

The range of instruments deployed by the centre – persuasion, pressure and control – was significant, the intention being to create a decisive shift in the balance of educational power so as to facilitate the prime aim of restructuring the service:

> The Education Act 1980, the block grant system, the school curriculum initiative and the planned reductions in the Government's financial support for education represent when taken together an actual or potential diminution of LEA discretion. . . . Looking at the education service as a whole, it seems that the DES acting on its own initiative and in the context of more general government policies, is now in the process of expanding its influence at the expense of LEAs.

Accountability

Centralized control of education would, it was proposed, enable the service to become more accountable to the nation for the resources it consumed: 'Education, like any other public service, is answerable to the society which it serves and which pays for it' (DES, 1977a, p. 2). The Green Paper *Education in Schools* argued that 'Growing recognition of the need for schools to demonstrate their accountability to the society which they serve requires a coherent and soundly based means of assessment for the education system as a whole, for schools and for individual pupils' (DES, 1977a, p. 16). At national level, the role of HMI would be strengthened to describe and assess educational performance of local education. They would be expected to work in a complementary way with LEA advisory services: 'both in different ways are accountable and need to understand how their similar but complementary responsibilities fit together in the interest of the system. Qualitative assessment would be complemented by qualitative analysis and a national "account" of educational achievement would be developed by a new Assessment of Performance Unit [APU].'

At local level accountability could be strengthened if the LEAs developed more sophisticated systems for assessing and presenting accounts of performance:

> Local Education Authorities need to be able to assess the relative performance of their school to reach decisions about staffing, the allocation of resources and other matters. In particular, it is an essential facet of their accountability for educational standards that they must be able to identify schools which consistently perform poorly, so that appropriate remedial action can be taken. Such assessment will take account of examination and test results, but will also depend heavily on a detailed knowledge of the circumstances of the schools by the authorities' officers, their inspectors and advisers, and such self assessment as may be undertaken by the schools. There is scope here for the authorities to try to achieve a greater degree of uniformity in their approach to the assessment of schools. But 'league tables' of school performance based on examination or standardised test results in isolation can be seriously misleading because they fail to take account of other important factors such as the wide differences between school catchment areas. This danger will be recognised by local education authorities which are operating assessment practices (of whatever type) yielding results for their schools individually. Increasingly schools should assess their own performance against their own objectives as well as the external criteria. In so doing they may be expected to keep under review much information useful to their governors, the local authority and HM Inspectorate.
>
> (DES, 1977a, p. 17)

At the level of schools and pupils, the Government encouraged the development of as much information as possible about pupil achievement in order to be able to assess how they were progressing: questioning, testing, internal school examining and diagnostic assessment were recommended to improve the record, the account, of achievement. Information tied together the relationship of power and accountability, providing the state with the knowledge that would allow it to rationalize its planning.

RATIONALIZATION

The management of contraction necessitated the national reduction of resources to education and thus the need for the service radically to review and rationalize its resource distribution. The possibilities for rationalization were indicated in declining school rolls, while the duplication of courses for the 16–19 age group and the inefficiencies in the use of resources between schools and colleges suggested that reorganization and rationalization would offer educational as well as financial advantages. Yet it was well understood in Whitehall in the late 1970s that underlying and defining any decisions about resource rationalization were questions of educational opportunity: in particular the proportion of any age group the Government was willing to continue to support in their education. The rationalization of 'surplus capacity' would clearly take a number of forms.

Policy-makers, especially in local government, were often ambivalent about surplus places: wanting both to eliminate them to save resources and to use them to extend parental choice of schools. In this period planned rationalization of resources always had the upper hand. A number of consultative papers were prepared by the DES between 1978 and 1980, encouraging local authorities to examine systematically 'the problems of rationalisation and cost effectiveness' (see DES, 1977c, 1979c, 1980b). The need for rationalization was expressed most clearly by the Macfarlane Committee in *Education for 16–19 Year Olds*, which brought together Government and Local

Authority Association representatives. The overriding strategy of rationalization took a number of interrelated forms, some expressed more explicitly than others.

Rationalizing institutions for resource efficiency

In a period of contracting numbers and financial resources governments argued that there are important educational as well as financial benefits to be gained by closing or amalgamating schools and thus adjusting the scale of institutional provision to reduce school rolls. The effective management of scarce resources was emphasized by the Macfarlane Committee but had its most forceful expression in Circular 2/81, which set out the financial case for removing surplus capacity of accommodation:

> The precise savings to be realised will vary according to local factors. But they will include reductions in heating, lighting and maintenance costs, as well as – for whole schools – teaching, administrative and caretaking costs. Every 100,000 surplus places taken out of use should on average yield savings approaching £10 million – excluding any savings on teachers' salaries.
>
> (p. 5)

Not to make such financial savings could only be at the expense of much-needed teachers, books and other educational resources. Indeed, the circular stressed educational arguments: 'a reduction in the number of permanent places can bring substantial educational benefits'. In secondary schools, closure and amalgamation would protect the curriculum and staffing – HMI (1979) having demonstrated the way the range of subjects became restricted when school size fell to three or four forms of entry. Particular subjects, such as science and languages, were especially vulnerable. Post-16, the disadvantages of small teaching group sizes became especially acute, and attempts to staff a full range of curricular opportunities were often achieved at the expense of provision in the lower school. There were, the circular maintained, 'powerful arguments in favour of educating 16–19 year olds in fairly large groups' (p. 4). The Government was arguing that rationalization of institutional provision would offer economies of scale that would not only yield financial savings and the realization of capital assets but also help significantly to maintain and improve the educational effectiveness of schools.

The question of optimum school size

Early analyses of the problem of managing falling school rolls tended to work with assumptions about school size taken from an earlier period: that comprehensive schools needed to be large if they were to offer the range of specialisms required by all children across the ability range. Briault and Smith (1980), for example, argued strongly for LEAs to reorganize their schools so as to establish 'the smallest reasonable number of secondary schools and the largest size of schools having in mind distances between schools' (p. 245). Their argument drew attention to

> a necessarily more restricted curriculum for the fourth and fifth years; the inevitability of mixed-ability groups; mixed or restricted objective groups for public examinations; greater difficulties in deploying staff in such a way as to use a teacher to the best advantage and yet still ensure that the curriculum is covered. A lower PTR is required, not

temporarily . . . but permanently to maintain the small school *per se*. . . . If excellence is the aim . . . then the peer learning group must be more than a handful. . . . I am not arguing that a small school is necessarily a poor school, simply that it has greater difficulties and disadvantages in meeting all the educational needs of all its pupils, which reflect not upon its teachers but which arise simply from its size.

(Briault and Smith, 1980, pp. 238–9)

This classic argument for a large comprehensive school was in line with that presented by the Secondary Heads Association (SHA) in its booklet *Big Is Beautiful* (SHA, 1979). Large, in this analysis, tended to mean schools with perhaps eight to ten 'forms of entry'.

Professional opinion began to move against very large schools, arguing that such a scale was not required to provide an adequate range of curricular experience and, in any event, providing only a 'few large schools' would deprive many communities of a school at a time when many were beginning to accept the significance for pupil achievement of close ties between teachers and parents. The argument of minimum size consented to five or six forms of entry as acceptable educationally:

Experience suggests . . . that 11–16 comprehensive schools of 4-form entry and below find it difficult to offer a curriculum of appropriate range and to provide sufficient teaching groups, without the support of staff : pupil teacher ratios much more generous than the average; such ratios may have to be achieved at the expense of the authority's larger secondary schools.

(DES Circular 2/81)

The problem in provision for 11–16 pupils was, therefore, maintaining schools of a sufficient size. Schools below five or six forms of entry found it increasingly difficult to deliver a broad curriculum without staff subsidization. The alternatives were to provide extra staff resources as rolls fell, to narrow curricular provision or to close and amalgamate schools in order to keep average school size up.

The greatest problems of contraction often appeared at sixth form level. *Better Schools* (DES, 1985) states that 'A comprehensive school catering for pupils aged 11–16 normally needs to be of a size which enables it to maintain a sixth form of at least 150, if it is to provide an adequate range of A level and other courses' (p. 80). Some teachers would argue that sixth forms could be effective at a smaller size. Nevertheless, after rising in the late 1970s and early 1980s sixth form teaching group sizes had begun to fall. In 1983, 55.3 per cent of classes had fallen to ten or fewer pupils. The Macfarlane Committee on Education for 16–19 Year Olds (DES, 1980c) argued persuasively for the virtues of size:

We think . . . that the size of the 16–19 group must be a primary consideration in the generality of cases. First there is the issue of the range of combination of subjects which can be offered. Attempts to increase that range beyond what the school can naturally support can lead to diversion of attention and resources from those in the lower school, to their immediate and longer term disadvantage. Next, we think it fair to assume that students are more likely to find stimulus in working together in a group rather than being spread in ones or twos over a number of institutions. Working together in larger groups they are more likely to appreciate the standards and expectations attaching to sixth form study and to draw support from their peers. Finally there is the matter of teaching quality and qualifications; larger groups can more easily justify in the first place and attract (and retain) a sufficient number of teachers of high calibre. We conclude that educational considerations point strongly though not without exception towards the concentration of 16–19 pupils and students into large groups.

(p. 28)

The Macfarlane Committee found, as one would expect, that the average group size was higher in sixth form colleges, at 11.6, than in comprehensive sixth forms, at 10.3. The study also found a positive correlation between group size and A level performance.

Rationalizing school and college

The process of rationalizing resources to ensure greater effectiveness of educational provision, especially for 16–19-year-olds, required the focus to shift beyond the closure or amalgamation of schools to the relationship between schools and further education colleges. Rationalizing of provision across the education sectors could eliminate waste and duplication of resources, introduce much-needed flexibility in the use of institutions and staff, and most importantly facilitate the new objective of developing a vocationally oriented curriculum by breaking down barriers between education and training.

These policy intentions were made clear in a series of consultative documents. In *Providing Educational Opportunities for 16–18 Year Olds* (DES, 1979c) the Government expressed concern at the unplanned overlap in provision between the sectors: 'commonly both school and FE sectors are concerned with providing for the 16–18's and often there is overlap between them . . . much duplication has undoubtedly occurred because of uncoordinated growth amongst institutions' (p. 3). The pressures upon resources and the need to make effective use of plant and teachers, and the requirements of students and employers all 'demand flexibility in structures and institutions' and suggest, in particular, that 'it may be necessary to ask whether the present boundaries between school and college are the right ones'. LEAs, as Macfarlane proposed, should review the totality of institutional provision in the 16–19 area and consider the scope for extended collaboration between school and college or seek to create new integrated institutions for 16–19-year-olds.

The educational as much as the economic argument for rationalizing school and college provision was given significant emphasis. The changing world of employment and the pressing demands of employers suggested a rationalization and redirection of the curriculum offered post-16. Traditional distinctions between training (specific vocational tasks) and education (the general development of knowledge, moral value and understanding) were now outmoded. The rationalization of the curriculum between school and college would allow 'the well recognised national need for more vocational education of a high standard in the face of major changes in the nature of employment' and enable the country to produce 'the skilled and versatile work-force needed for the future'.

The rationalization of opportunities

It was well understood, however, that rationalizing provision really presupposes qualitative policy decisions about educational opportunities; that is, about systematizing access to educational routes and thus to the labour market. The rationalization of resources presupposes the rationalization of educational offerings and opportunities. As the Treasury official insisted at an ESGE 16–19 sub-committee in 1979, for the members of the committee to determine how to rationalize educational resources they must first address themselves to the issue of *how much* opportunity, choice and access is to be allowed *to which* groups of young people: define desirable levels of participation first for the whole age group and then for the separate 16–19 'client groups'. The Macfarlane Report incorporated these arguments about the need to rationalize educational opportunities: what was offered in the past may now be unreasonable in cost as well as being unsuited to the nation's needs. The aspirations of young people must be realistic and rationalized from now on: 'that a range of opportunities is available of a quality that meets the realistic aspirations of young people, parents and society at a cost which the nation judges it right to pay'. The Mansell Report, as we have seen, also underlined the importance of realism.

The policy of rationalization of educational provision therefore had a number of dimensions. At the most obvious level rationalization meant reducing surplus capacity in school accommodation and thus promoting the efficient use of resources. The efficient rationalization of resources taken a stage further embraced colleges as well as schools, since the Department wished to systematize the use of resources as between school and college so as to prevent duplication and waste. Rationalization of the relationship between school and college, however, was designed to accomplish the integration of education and training provision rather than just the efficient use of resources. The economic objectives were a means to achieve educational policy objectives and to improve the relevance of education to the world of work. At this point the more complete rationalization plan is disclosed. Effective rationalization presupposed a tightening of the relationship between educational 'outputs' and the needs of society and economy through the systematizing of access and opportunity.

STRATIFICATION: FROM SYSTEM TO SOCIAL RATIONALIZATION

The progressive rationalization of educational planning had been a central part of corporate restructuring since the mid-1970s. The state believed that it required the necessary powers and steering capacity to redirect the education service during a period of change. The Department had been determined to eliminate what it regarded as an outmoded constitutional contradiction: its overriding duty to 'control and direct', while bereft of the necessary powers. Only, it contended, a more unified government of education with an integrated policy planning system could manage this changing context effectively – allowing it to compete with its rival in this period, that fast-moving juggernaut, the Manpower Services Commission. (The MSC, in fact provided a model and a rationale: the model was of a centralized bureaucracy, an effective centre–local delivery system; and a rationale that such a model was the only way to win resources at the Cabinet table – the MSC could deliver, the DES wasted time in consultation.)

Considerable strides were made towards the creation of an integrated planning system in education. Roles and responsibilities were being clarified, authority and discretion defined, inter-organizational machinery developed and policy instruments for steering capacity designed. Departmental control was not yet realized, but the trend was unmistakeably towards centralization and concentration of power. Unlike other corporate policy planning developments of the time (see Leach *et al.*, 1983; Skelcher *et al.*, 1983; Hinings *et al.*, 1983) it had, however, been a step-wise, incremental, less open development, fitting the pieces of the system together discretely over time. Arguably this had been because of the nature of the policy sector – its scale, complexity and diversity – and, perhaps, because of the nature of the purposes to which the system would be directed.

The concern had been to weaken local government and the profession in schools and the LEA. If, however, we are to account for the strategies designed to control and direct local education and to erode the authority of its principal vehicle, local government, we need to examine other deeper-seated causes and purposes of educational policy planning than the management of surplus capacity in schools.

The restructuring and systematization of education had been directed to economic and socio-political change. The rationalization of resources was important, but not the exclusive factor. The cuts made the efficient use of resources a priority: half-empty schools and the duplication of provision between school and college waste scarce resources and restrict the quality of the circular offering (see Walsh *et al.*, 1984). Yet it was well understood by policy-makers that the rationalization of resources really presupposed more fundamental decisions about the range of opportunities that were to be provided.

To this end, the Macfarlane Committee believed that it was appropriate to define more clearly than hitherto what should count as a reasonable or suitable range of opportunities for 16–19-year-olds. Opportunities, they argued, should be seen in relation to the educational and training (or the vocational) needs of different 'client groups'. The Committee classified these groups as comprising the different routes taken by young people at 16: for example, those who entered employment, those who were without work or the prospect of work, those who pursued A level courses, those who sought specifically vocational qualifications in TEC and BEC, or the 'new sixth' who returned to education without any clear vocational or educational objective. Distinct groups could therefore be distinguished and differentiated in educational needs and opportunities – 'it is that young people should branch out at the age of 16, each according to his or her abilities, aptitudes and career intentions'. Macfarlane was concerned to erase status distinctions between these different vocational routes and thus to promote 'even-handedness of treatment' and 'parity of esteem' between them.

The policy of rationalizing opportunities and encouraging realism of aspirations was not being left to exhortation or chance. The chosen vehicle was to construct sharply differentiated curricular routes that steered young people along different tracks into alternative employment. In the past, 16–19 provision was demand-led in the long term and resource-led in the short term; in the future it would be curriculum-led. How much education (the questions of access and opportunity or the desirable levels of participation) should be offered was then a matter to be decided 'internally' by the circular paths that young people would become locked into. The strategy had been to identify separate 'client groups' that possessed ostensibly significant differences in ability and, therefore, had alternative 'needs' that purportedly required different provision. It was the language of classification and streaming:

> young people should branch out at the age of 16, each according to his or her abilities.
>
> (DES, 1980c, p. 17)

> there will be increasing differentiation of routes at 16; the academic A level route will become more intensive academic and a jolly good thing too. Within each stream there will be different but intensive provision. There will be some switching of courses – about as much as there was between the secondary moderns and the grammar schools.
>
> (Senior DES official)

we have been concerned throughout with the need to promote even-handedness of treatment and parity of esteem within 16–19 education.

(DES, 1980c, p. 18)

The rationalization of opportunities, together with a vocationalized and classified curriculum, amounted to a more overt stratification of young people than we had previously witnessed. The language of tripartite education – parity of esteem between modern, technical and grammar sectors – having been almost eliminated from the secondary sector, reappeared in the tertiary sector. Government officials, particularly in the Inspectorate, were talking of three client groups (identifying teams with functional responsibilities for each sector). The tertiary modern group would comprise young people on MSC courses (YOP, YTS and YT) and on the DES 17 plus pre-vocational courses; the tertiary technical group would comprise those on the more advanced TEC and BEC courses together with those who were to be selected into the new MSC-controlled technical stream courses (TEI); the tertiary grammar group would comprise those doing A levels and beginning university courses. The 17 plus vocational courses were to have their own internal forms of differentiation. As one senior HMI put it, the 'technical', 'business' and 'general' modules were conceived as selective streams for a hierarchy of ability: 'having divided the age group into sheep and goats, we will then divide the goats into those with horns and those without'.

The 16–19 framework of courses and assessment was being used to vocationalize, rationalize and stratify the age group in order to fit young people into the developing needs of the economy and of employment. This streaming was believed by some officials to be an important precondition for economic recovery during a period of rapid technological change: a fast stream was needed to help the nation compete effectively. Bernstein (1975) argued that there is no necessary subordination of education to the requirements of economic production, but suggested that the mode of production is anterior to the mode of education, and that when the systemic linkage between the two is strong then the stronger is the grip of the modes of production upon the structuring of education. The curriculum, however, plays a critical role in reproducing not only the skills required in differentiated layers of the labour market, but also the dispositions, the 'cultural capital' necessary for maintaining the structure and relations of the economic system (see Bourdieu and Passeron, 1977; Apple, 1979, 1982).

These curriculum changes were being designed, as one notable Chief Education Officer argued, to 'facilitate social control as much as encourage manpower planning'. The simple economic argument, therefore, that education was producing differentiated skills for a stratified labour market, was incomplete. It requires to be complemented and rounded out with a more developed argument about the social and political order. Both Labour and Conservative Governments seemed concerned as much about the social and political consequences of oversupply of highly educated young people (surplus social capacity) in a period of contracting job opportunities as they were about ostensible shortages of certain industrial skills. Writers such as Boudon (1974) and Hirsch (1977) noted the tendency of oversupply in education to produce not only queuing but also frustration, disappointment and potentially alienation. The consequences were not lost on the state's policy-makers:

by making continued full-time education the norm, we may be encouraging unrealistic career aspirations among young people.

(Labour Minister, reported in *Education*, 1977)

To offer young people advanced education but not thereafter the work opportunities to match their career aspirations is to offer them a false prospectus.

(Senior DES official)

There has to selection because we are beginning to create aspirations which increasingly society cannot match. In some ways this points to the success of education in contrast to the public mythology which as been created. When young people drop off the education production line and cannot find work at all, or work which does not meet their abilities or expectations, then we are only creating frustration with perhaps disturbing social consequences. We have to select: to ration the educational opportunities to meet the job opportunities so that society can cope with the output of education.

(ESGS 16–19 sub-group Representative)

We are in a period of considerable social change. There may be social unrest, but we can cope with the Toxteths. But if we have a highly educated and idle population we may possibly anticipate more serious social conflict. People must be educated once more to know their place.

(DES official)

The motivating concern here was about the nature of the polity as much as the economy. The impending structural changes to the economy were raising issues about the distribution of work and thus of wealth and power in society. How education was structured would result in different responses to these social issues and thus the nature of the political order. The lineages of the current restructuring of education were, however, unmistakeably clear. The state was developing modes of control in education that permitted closer scrutiny and direction of the social order.

The restructuring of education – of the curriculum and thus access to knowledge, of institutional opportunities and of selective certification for a layered labour market – had sought to redraw the boundaries of the social order by defining more precisely the place and horizons of its members. Policy planning systems defined a framework of status, roles and relations of participation in the chosen policy for the planning of change. In education as in other services, such planning was about the management of particular policies and resources over time. But in education, at least at historical and strategic moments, policy planning always expressed more fundamental political conflicts about the nature of society and polity, about the status and rules of participation and citizenship.

Educational policy planning was at the heart of the post-war social contract between the state, capital and labour (a contract to offer employment, income, opportunity and citizenship in exchange for the retention of the mixed economy), offering the prospect of opportunity and social advance in an open society (see Gellner, 1983). The vehicle of opportunities as well as welfare services was local government. Now, by regulating more directly the capacities and horizons of young people, planning sought to produce an alternative social classification, a Platonic order of control through differentiation. The rationalizing of the state – and thus the weakening of local government – had been defined as a precondition for this period of social control and restructuring.

TOWARDS STEERING CAPACITY

The corporate state sought to empower Whitehall to facilitate restructuring. The strategies seemed to confirm the account of Salter and Tapper (1981), who described the increasing centralization of educational powers. A tendency had been established, significant inroads had been achieved, but we would need to wait a little longer before we could say definitely with Salter and Tapper that the DES dominated and, increasingly, controlled the process of educational change. The increase was significant, as they argued, but did not yet amount to control (in Weber's sense of will achieved despite resistance).

The achievements in particular fields of policy had been slow, incomplete, uneven and incremental. Significant gains were nevertheless made in the underlying agenda of restructuring. The Department had been successful in creating an ethos, a new climate of values that reinforced vocationalism and realism. Glennerster argued that central government had its most effective impact on the 'value climate and the rules of debate' (Glennerster, 1983; see also Stewart, 1983). It was arguable that the DES achieved more than this. It supervised the contraction of the service and with the reduction of numbers into higher education the rationalization of opportunities had begun. Markedly differentiated curriculum tracks, facilitating the stratification of opportunity, were now being firmly laid down. In general the ground rules for the new education system were being established.

But the agenda of restructuring was beyond the powers presently available to the state. Frustration with the slow pace of change in conjunction with the competition of the MSC accentuated the DES's concern about the contradictions within the 1944 Act that obstructed its progress. Section 1, it argued, was the most important constitutional principle underlying the educational system and had to be reinforced if the necessary changes were to be secured. The DES sought more power.

Chapter 5

Education in the Market Place

RIGHTS AND CHOICE IN A NEW SOCIAL ORDER

A Conservative Government elected in 1979 on a manifesto promoting the rights of individuals signalled the demise of corporatism. Although the agenda of stratifying educational opportunity would remain, the new right believed that the institution of the market would more effectively realize the restructuring of education than any detailed systems of national policy or manpower planning, while giving the impression that the outcomes had been chosen by the people. The agenda of strengthening the state would also remain, but now hidden behind the mask of 'social choice'.

The Conservatives have since 1979 placed before Parliament a historically unique torrent of legislation to rewrite the governance of education. Its driving obsession is to wipe out any lingering infection of social democracy as much as to create a new polity that expresses and organizes an alternative vision of education and society. The ideas that informed the previous era are now anathema: the pursuit of *equality* of opportunity, through *comprehensive schools* and colleges, conceived of as a whole *system*, a seamless web of learning and opportunity, and *planned* by local education authorities through their *professional* communities. The whole purpose of education had, it was claimed, been distorted by a mistaken preoccupation with social engineering and egalitarianism: education is intrinsically individual and inequality of achievement inescapable. A vision of a consumer democracy was needed to replace these purported failures of the social democratic and corporate state that had lasted for a generation and more into the 1970s.

Individuals are not equal, the new right argues, but different, and their rights to develop their inherited capacity and property are inalienable, outweighing any claims of redistributive justice. Rawls's belief that inherited skill forms a common asset to mankind is unintelligible according to this perspective. We are led to believe that 'there is no such thing as society'. 'There are only individual people with their own individual lives' (Nozick, 1974) and the benefit of all is best achieved when each is allowed to pursue his or her self-interest in competition with others in the market place. The legitimacy of this moral order derives not only from its protection of individual interests but also from enabling freedom of choice. The values encourage an active polity, whose members are not conceived of as passive, dependent subjects but as agents reflecting upon and actively developing their interests. Government is made to serve and account to the market place.

The role of the minimal state is to protect the liberty of individual choice by maximizing the area around individuals that is 'free from' external constraint and interference. The 'welfare state', it is claimed, was mistaken both in trying to create equality, and in denying individuals the right to choose created a sense of dependency among citizens. The polity, by empowering the professionals and providers at the expense of the public, denied the possibility of consumer choice and accountability. A society in transition would benefit by according the greatest possible freedom of individuals to develop their self-interest and advantage. An empowered public could replace the burdensome and self-interested bureaucracy of the welfare state. The central vehicle for the new consumer democracy is the market, which through the competition it generates will, it is claimed, enhance the quality of goods and services provided. What is the market and how does this essentially economic institution fare when introduced into the public domain?

MARKETS

The market allows many buyers and sellers to exchange goods and services through voluntary transactions uncoordinated by any planning authority. In the 'neoclassical' model (Marshall, 1936), supply and demand are mediated and balanced by prices which, although the unintended outcome of previous market interactions, provide the participants with information that allows them rationally to calculate their advantage and decide how to act. The price mechanism, therefore, offers the crucial signal in this 'spontaneous' exchange: acting, as Levacic (1991) suggests, as 'the unseen hand (a kind of social auctioneer)' to inform and clear the market. This 'classical' market is held to work most effectively when many buyers and sellers are free to compete and none can control the ruling price. The operation of 'perfect competition' ensures the most efficient allocation of societies' resources, the exchanges reaching an equilibrium position when no one person can be made better off without another being made worse off (so-called Pareto optimality). Monopoly is the enemy of the purely competitive market.

Levacic argues that this neoclassical perspective should not be seen as the only model of market operation. There are others. The neo-Austrian approach illustrated by Krizner (1973) offers an alternative approach to understanding entrepreneurial competition:

> With the neo-Austrian position – often termed the 'competitive process' approach – the market is seen as a *process* of selection, turmoil and change where *dis*equilibrium conditions prevail. This is an overtly dynamic theory of the market. Less emphasis is placed upon price and more on the (beneficial) effects of the competitive process that markets engender.
>
> (Levacic, 1991)

There is nothing intrinsically wrong with monopoly according to this perspective because it may reflect successful entrepreneurial initiative, risk taking and investment that have provided a competitive edge in the market. Such firms should be allowed to profit from their dynamism. A longer-term view of the market will place the social costs of market imperfections – restrictive practices, monopolies, limited information and rationality – in perspective: for in time the competitive rigours engendered by markets will favour rival producers and deconstruct monopoly power. The sovereign power of consumers, moreover, creates an inexorable pressure in favour of efficiency and quality, driving poor producers to the wall.

This analysis is consistent with Hayek's. Hayek (1973, 1976, 1979) has been a key influence upon the Government's reforms. The order of the market is to be valued because it produces collective good from the free agency of individuals. No other institution could coordinate actions with the same flexibility and thus efficiency in adapting scarce resources to demand. No centralized planning authority could acquire the information or knowledge that emerges spontaneously through exchange and allows individuals to make appropriate adaptations to their behaviour. In this way the market provides the most effective process of learning about changing circumstances in a context of uncertainty and thus, by promoting initiative while holding centralized authority at bay, protects individual liberty. The state is 'the road to serfdom', the market the source of freedom. The outcomes of the market, because they emerge from impersonal transactions, can only be regarded as impartial and fair. There is in any event, given a diversity of human wants that makes impossible the construction of any single preference order, no mechanism of reconciling competing ends other than market place struggle.

Inequality, Hayek believes, is an intrinsic quality of market exchange. Some individuals will be better entrepreneurs, calculating risks and advantages more effectively than their competitors. They should properly garner greater rewards for their skill and effort. Ambition based on market merit should accrue material advantage. The ensuing inequality can only benefit society by promoting progress through competition.

Even though markets seek to impose limits upon the power of 'the central authority', they are an institution that is inescapably, like others, underwritten by the state. Markets presuppose a legal framework that establishes laws of individual freedom of exchange and contract and guarantees rights of property. Although the effectiveness of the market grows out of an interplay of competing self-interest, 'exchange is possible only in a society in which a moral code and authority keep social peace' (Lindblom, 1977): that competitors do not deceive each other, that they honour contracts and that losers will respect the winners' appropriations of profit. But then the minimal state has never left order to moral probity. Social control has always gone hand in hand with the market order. Bentham's nightwatchman state protected private property and the rule of law by developing powers to monitor and withdraw social 'misfits' who might disturb the equilibrium of the market order. The surveillance of the panopticon had its place.

These institutional conditions required for any competitive exchange point up the reality that markets are social constructions, constituted to serve particular and often political purposes. This is especially apparent when the commodity model is applied to goods and services that do not strictly meet the criteria of the private transaction in the market. Private goods are those whose benefits can be enjoyed by those who own them to the exclusion of others. Goods are termed 'public' when they 'do not fit into the normal assumption in law that property rights are exclusive and transferable or the normal assumption in economics that goods and services can be provided by voluntary market exchanges' (Hood, 1986). Public goods are defined by economists as possessing, first, 'non-excludability'. It is impossible, ineffecient or impracticable to exclude consumers from the benefits of the goods and services once they are provided. It is therefore not possible to charge for them (for example, street lighting). Second, public goods possess 'non-rivalness' or indivisibility of benefit, where one person's consumption does not reduce the amount available to others (e.g. crossing a bridge).

Public goods, therefore, are collective goods. Provided for one they are necessarily provided for all. The public domain will take responsibility for providing the goods and services that individuals cannot (or will not) provide and that are regarded as essential to maintaining 'the common wealth'. It may be defending the boundaries of the realm, or regulating hygiene and thus public health, or producing the physical infrastructure of roads and street lighting that are chosen because their characteristics require public decision and expenditure if they are to happen.

Although these defining characteristics of public goods appear quite clear, deciding whether a good has the characteristics, and whether to provide it, is a value-laden and necessarily political choice. A number of goods or services are what Laver (1986) calls 'hybrid': they have both private and public characteristics. Health care and education are consumed by individuals and are services as such, which can be charged for while additional consumption raises marginal costs. Yet inoculating against infectious diseases or creating an educated democracy can clearly be defined as goods that are consumed by all and benefit the public at large. Thus,

> though the characteristics defining public goods are quite precise the goods which possess these characteristics may not be clearly defined until some agreement is reached as to the benefits they provide. . . . The decision about which goods are public goods may be dependent on a judgement about the value of the benefit to others: it may thus be a 'political decision'.
>
> (Foster *et al.*, 1980)

The technical definition of what is to count as a public good can conceal the necessity of collective judgement and political choice. The political task of constructing the hybrid market in education has involved a programme of legislation over 15 years. A senior civil servant proposed that the emerging framework of governance for education might best be interpreted as forming an 'administered market'.

DESIGNING AN ADMINISTERED MARKET

The Government has over time created a distinctive framework to expand consumer choice and influence at the expense of the providers. Consumers are empowered to choose among competing schools but the market is at the same time highly regulated by an increasingly authoritarian state that controls the rules of exchange. Yet the concentration of central power and the increasing scope for competitive individualism are designed to interact to alter fundamentally the structure and purpose of education, eroding the authority of the engine of social democratic order – local government.

Three key phases of development can be identified: beginning in 1980 with parents being encouraged to express their preferences for schools, consolidated with the 1986 and 1988 Education Acts formalizing the mechanisms of choice and constraint, and (perhaps) completed by the 1993 Act, which sets in train processes that deconstruct the local system of education.

The 1980 Education Act: the principle of parental choice

Both Labour and Conservative Governments (1976–80) wanted, especially in a time of resource constraint, to rationalize educational provision but also to make political gains by allowing parents more say in their choice of school. The number of parents who were appealing to the Secretary of State over the school their children had been allocated to by the LEA had increased from about 100 per year before comprehensivization to about 1,000 a year by the mid-1970s.

It was, however, the Conservative Party that was from the first more committed to parental choice, because it sat more consistently with Conservatives' beliefs in individual rights. In 1974 the Opposition spokesman on education, Norman St John-Stevas, announced 'A Charter of Parents' Rights' that was as much a response to the 'Black Paper' right wing of his party as to the supposed dissatisfaction of parents unable to choose schools. The Charter was included in the Conservatives' October 1974 Election Manifesto:

> A Charter of Parents' Rights: An important part of the distinctive Conservative policy on Education is to recognise parental rights. A say in how their children are to be brought up is an essential ingredient in the parental role. We will introduce additional rights for parents. First, by amending the 1944 Education Act, we will impose clear obligations on the State and local authorities to take account of the wishes of parents. Second, we will consider establishing a local appeal system for parents dissatisfied with the allotment of schools.

By 1976, the Conservative Party had extended the Charter to include parental choice of school. As Tweedie (1986) and Stillman (1986) point out in their analyses, the bases of the Conservative rationale had moved beyond notions of individual freedom and responsibility to tie choice into a theory about the quality of schooling: consumer choice and market forces would reinforce 'good' schools and close those that were failing; choice would lead to greater parental control of education; and, as some Conservatives appreciated, choice would inevitably lead to academic and social selection, with over-subscribed schools being able to pick and choose which pupils they wanted to admit. The Conservative Manifesto of 1979 reflected the shift in thinking:

> Extending parents' right and responsibilities, including their right of choice, will also help raise standards by giving them greater influence over education. Our parents' charter will place a clear duty on government and local authorities to take account of parents' wishes when allocating children to schools, with a local appeal system for those dissatisfied. Schools will be required to publish prospectuses giving details of their examination and other results.

The Conservative Party won the 1979 election committed to reducing public expenditure – for example, by eliminating surplus school capacity – but also to extending parents' rights to choice, which, in education, depended upon the existence of some spare capacity.

The dilemmas for LEAs of reconciling parental choice and efficient provision – of markets and rational plans – became constituted in the enabling legislation: the 1980 Education Act. The Act articulated the new Conservative Government's perspective on the dilemma of managing contraction and yet enabling parental choice. On a superficial reading, the Act appears to be a rather nondescript collection of disparate items, a miscellany of trifles. Yet it began to challenge the organizing principles in the government of education that had lasted since the 1944 Education Act, which emphasized local administration within a national service. Although the general principle governing the Act proposed that 'pupils [were] to be educated in accordance with the wishes of their parents', ostensibly affording them a direct and significant influence in the government of education, the most influential of the partners was the local education authority, and its power grew through the 1950s and 1960s.

The effect of several provisions in the 1980 Education Act was to weaken the authority of the LEA to plan and manage local education. The new Secretary of State, Mark Carlisle, did not go as far as some members of his party would have wanted – to give parents the right of unrestricted choice – realizing that LEAs did require some levers to help them manage falling school rolls. Nevertheless, the legislation strengthened the influence of parents.

Whereas Labour had prepared *statutory* PALs (planned admission limits), section 8 of the 1980 Act merely allowed LEAs to publish limits as their planning guidelines, which would enable them to manage local education efficiently. But LEA powers were weakened further in two ways. First, by parents: section 6 stated the general presumption that LEAs must comply with parental preferences for schools unless they could demonstrate that admission would prejudice efficient education because of the extra expenditure incurred. The legal adviser to one large LEA argued in a public seminar that according to this interpretation of the law a local authority would find it almost impossible to exclude a child because the authority would not be able to prove that *one* further admission prejudiced efficiency. And each preference had to be taken individually so that even if there were a whole extra class in the admissions queue each claim had to be taken separately and considered on its own merits. In practice the courts have not taken this interpretation.

The same rules of individual assessment would apply to parents who appealed against the LEA admission decision. Section 7 of the Act stated that 'every LEA shall make arrangements for enabling parents to appeal against' the decision of the LEA or, in the case of the voluntary schools, of the governing body. To review such appeals it would be the duty of the LEA to constitute a new 'appeal committee', which would not be chaired by a member of the LEA, although the LEA might maintain a majority on the panel if it so chose. The decision of the committee was binding on the LEA.

In order to help parents make their decision about which school to choose, it would be the duty of the LEA, for each of its schools, to publish information that could inform their choices. The information would include not only the admission arrangements but also, by regulation of the Secretary of State, information on the education provided in each school as well as its achievements, including examination results. The research of Stillman and Maychell (1986) indicated that the number of appeals had grown year by year since 1980, up to 10,000 in 1983: 'In respect of appeals the interpretation of parents' rights is evolving rapidly and the balance between parents' individual wishes and the broader needs of society is still moving toward the parent' (p. 188). The data are more equivocal about trends of actual parental movement in the school market place. The studies of Stillman and Maychell (1986) and of Echols *et al.* (1990) suggest, however, that where LEAs vigorously promote parental choice, parents can pursue and gain the school of their preference.

The second way in which the 1980 Education Act weakened the authority of the LEA was by strengthening the power of the Secretary of State. Section 15 granted ministers the power to intervene and control admission limits should LEAs wish to change them significantly. Where an LEA intends to reduce the number of pupils in any relevant age group who are to be admitted to the school in any school year to a number that is four-fifths or less than four-fifths of the standard number (1979 intakes) applying under this section to the school in relation to that year and age group, it must submit to the Secretary of State its proposal for his or her approval. As rolls fell from the 1979 figure, emerging spare places could allow 'controlled' parental choice, with the Secretary of State having strengthened powers to regulate the balance of planning and choice between LEAs and parents. One DES official acknowledged that section 15 was a considerable increase in the powers of the centre (Ranson, 1985b).

The 1980 Education Act introduced important but limited change. Pressure groups on the right of the Conservative Party became impatient for more radical reform of the education service and through their political pamphlets successfully articulated the education ideology of consumer rights and market competition that was to shape the 1988 Education Reform Act.

The 1988 Education Reform Act: enabling competition

The ideologues of competition

The failures of education, it is argued, derive from the fact that professionals and (local) politicians seek to appropriate control of the service from its proper source – the parents. The 'producers' have taken over and pursue their own purposes at the expense of the needs of the 'consumers' of the service. The Adam Smith Institute's (1984) *Omega File* on education generalizes the problems facing education, in common with other state monopolies, as those of 'producer capture': 'whereby the service comes to be organised more to suit the needs of producers than consumers'. The professionals create a technical language that serves only to bamboozle ordinary people and they organize the system for their convenience rather than to respond to the demands of its consumers. The result is inertia and resistance to change.

The pamphleteers call for action and change: 'nothing short of radical measures are needed to improve the state maintained system of education and to placate its growing critics, the parents, the employers and the children themselves' (Sexton, 1987). The solution lies in new values and beliefs about education and the reconstitution of the government of education to suit.

The values emphasize that the education system must be built upon the principles of public choice and accountability. Individual parents have an inalienable right to choose the education their children receive. The values articulate beliefs about educational achievement which assert that a system which is accountable and responsive to the choices of individual consumers of the service will improve in quality as a necessary consequence. As in other forms of market exchange, the products that thrive can do so only because they have the support of consumers. Products that fail the test of the market place go out of business. The astringent experience of the market can be the test of quality in schooling as much as in the production of chocolate bars.

For consumers to fulfil their allotted role as quality controllers in the market place they require some diversity of product, information about the scope of choice and the quality of performance, as well as the opportunity to choose. If schools were made to respond to the market,

> there would be a built-in mechanism to raise standards and change forms and types of education in accordance with that market demand. . . . In short, it supposes that the wisdom of parents separately and individually exercised, but taken together becoming the collective wisdom is more likely to achieve higher standards more quickly and more acceptably to the public that the collective wisdom of the present bureaucrats, no matter how well meaning those bureaucrats may be.
>
> (Sexton, 1987, p. 9)

Creating this direct accountability between consumer and producer is the secret, it is argued, to renewal in education. To shift from a producer-led to a consumer-led system will take time but placing public choice at the heart of the system will release the quality that is alleged to be at present submerged under the weight of administration. Radical reforms are proposed to the government of education in order to reconstitute it according to these new organizing principles and values.

The pamphleteers propose to dismantle the present system of education government. For some, even the Department for Education (DFE) will become 'superflous' over a period of time as the routines of the market establish themselves. The *Omega File*, however, envisaged a continuing and strengthened role for HM Inspectorate to ensure that standards are maintained and teaching is of an acceptable quality. For the Hillgate Group, the state becomes an essential guarantor of the nation's traditional culture and values, 'safeguarding our educational tradition . . . a repository of knowledge, an inheritance that survives only if it is enshrined in durable institutions which have the means and purpose to pass it on' (Hillgate Group, 1986, p. 8).

A variety of strong, increasingly independent institutions is proposed, which will provide a differentiated system of education that will allow diversity of choice for parents. The independent sector would be reinforced, the direct grant schools recreated, 'magnet' and city technology schools established, grammar and secondary moderns restored *de facto*.

The root of the current problems, argue the pamphleteers, lies with the LEAs, which should be stripped of their powers and eliminated from the system of education government. In time, it is proposed, the ownership of all schools and the management of teachers should transfer to independent trusts or boards. This would create self-governing institutions under the control of parent governors and subject to consumer pressures in the market place. The survival of schools 'should depend on their ability to satisfy their customers. And their principal customers are parents, who should therefore be free to place their custom where they wish in order that educational institutions should be shaped, controlled and nourished by their demand' (Hillgate Group, 1986, p. 7). Strengthening the rights of individual consumers is the secret of improved educational quality.

The legislation

The Education Act was a radical recasting of the education service, constituting in its proposals many of the principles and values of the new liberalism outlined above. The Conservative reforms, it was claimed, would enhance achievement, improve school management and empower parents. The key to raising standards lay in the reform of government. Three principal strategies have informed the reconstruction of powers and responsibilities. The central idea has been that of *market formation*, the objective of which is to increase public choice through two means: (a) empowering active consumer participation by providing parents with information for accountability, the right to choose, appeal and register complaints and the opportunity to play a leading role in initiating and running new grant maintained schools; and (b) differentiating the governance of education by deregulating local government control (for example, of admissions and resource redistribution) and fostering competition by increasing the diversity of institutional types within an internal market. A second key idea has been to create *the responsive institution*. Schools are granted enhanced opportunities through local management to achieve autonomy and hence flexibility in the way they deploy resources, staff and their distinctive identities. The third strategy has involved *national regulation*, whereby schools would be subject to a planned curriculum that improved entitlement and standards for all by a better definition of what is taught and learnt.

The Bill presented to Parliament on 20 November 1987 conformed closely to a series of consultative papers published during the summer of that year. The Bill can be seen as the culmination of a decade's campaigning to strengthen the rights of parents in the government of education. The pamphleteers' proposals were now within the precincts of Parliament. Introducing the Bill in Parliament, the Secretary of State said:

> The Bill will galvanise parental involvement in schools. Parents will have more choice. They will have greater variety of schools of choose from. We will create new types of schools. Parents will be far better placed to know what their children are being taught and what they are learning. . . . And the Bill will introduce competition into the public provision of education. This competition will introduce a new dynamic into our schools system which will stimulate better standards all round.
>
> (DES, 1987a)

Parent power in a market place of schools that are made more accountable to their consumers would improve educational standards. Yet in the transformed system of government the Education Secretary realized the lost powers of 'control and direction', institutions were strengthened and the LEAs diminished. I shall review the Act's provisions in terms of their implications for the constituencies of education decision-making.

Parents were brought centre-stage in the establishing of an education market place. Parents were accorded choice, influence over governing bodies and control – if they chose – of new grant-maintained schools. 'Open' enrolment was designed to end the LEAs' capacity to place artificial limits on admission to schools. 'The government is committed to securing wider parental choice within the system of state schools.' To this end schools would be allowed to recruit up to their available capacity, defined as physical capacity or 'the standard number' admitted in 1979 (when schools were largely full) or, if it was higher, the number admitted in the year before the legislation took effect. If a governing body decided it wished to accept a larger number of pupils it could apply to the Secretary of State. Moreover, local electors could object to the Education Secretary if they believed an LEA had set the limit too low.

Parents were to acquire a determining influence over school governing bodies. The 1986 Education (No. 2) Act gave parents an equal representation with the LEA on governing bodies. Now the Act gave governors responsibilities for school budgets and the appointment and dismissal of staff, as well as the ability to overrule an LEA on redeployment of staff. The Act extended such proposals to the governing bodies of colleges. The representation of college consumers – for example, business and commerce – was increased 'to ensure that the governing body is, and is seen to be, properly independent of the maintaining LEA'.

Parents were to be granted the capacity to acquire control of schools if they chose:

> The Government is taking action to increase the autonomy of schools and their respon-siveness to parental wishes. . . . The Government considers that it should . . . respond to the numerous indications it has received that groups of parents want responsibility of running their schools as individual institutions. It proposes to provide an additional route to autonomy by introducing legislation . . . to enable governors of county and voluntary maintained schools, with the support of parents, to apply to the Secretary of State for maintenance by grant from Central Government, instead of maintenance by LEAs. The Government believes that this proposal . . . will add a new and powerful dimension to the ability of parents to exercise choice within the publicly provided sector of education. The greater diversity of provision which will result should enhance the prospect of improv-ing education standards in all schools. Parents and local communities would have new opportunities to secure the development of their schools in ways appropriate to the needs of their children and in accordance with their wishes, within the legal framework of a national curriculum.
>
> (DES, 1987c)

These schools would receive grant directly from the Secretary of State so as to form a new type of independent school within the maintained sector and, initially at least, they would retain their existing form (a comprehensive could not opt out and imme-diately become a grammar school). Governors of the larger primary schools as well as of all county and voluntary secondary schools could apply to opt out but only if they already had the support of 20 per cent of parents from a secret postal ballot. Parents, if necessary, could override the opposition of governors and pursue their own applica-tion according to the same rules. Parents would have a determining influence on the governing bodies of newly formed grant-maintained (GM) schools.

Other independent schools, known as city technology colleges (CTCs), would accom-pany GM schools in creating much greater variety of institutions for parents to choose from in the market place. As McLeod (1988) described, CTCs would be established by the Secretary of State, who 'may enter into agreement with any person' to provide such urban schools. They would offer free education for pupils of different abilities with a broad curriculum, given an emphasis on science and technology. CTCs had more discre-tion in relation to the National Curriculum than other LEA schools, although they had broadly to adhere to it as a condition of receiving grant.

Schools and colleges were to be granted more autonomy so that they could become more responsive and accountable to their consumers. As Thomas (1989) analysed, the Act proposed to delegate financial responsibilities to school governors:

> (i) to ensure that parents and the community know on what basis the available resources are distributed in their area and how much is spent on each school
>
> (ii) to give the governors of all county and voluntary secondary schools and of larger primary schools freedom to take expenditure decisions which match their own priorities and the guarantee that their own school will benefit if they achieve efficiency savings.
>
> (DES, 1987b)

LEAs would be required to submit 'schemes' to the Secretary of State which would describe how they proposed to delegate financial resources to schools, including the allocation formula to be used. Parents would be able to assess the efficiency of each school because

> at the end of each year the LEA would be required to publish information on actual expenditure at each school which could be compared to the original plans. This information together with that required of governors relating to the achievement of the national curriculum would provide the basis on which parents could evaluate whether best use had been made of the resources available to the governors.
>
> (DES, 1987b)

Colleges, too, were to be governed by equivalent formula funding arrangements and performance indicators were to be used to assess their efficiency.

In the past, the allocation of resources had been a closed professional affair. Now it was likely that the criteria as well as the distribution of resources would become a subject of public debate, as consumers enquired why one institution received more than another or was more efficient than another.

If consumers were to express their preferences in the market place then their choices needed to be informed. Strategic direction was given to the new system through proposals for the Education Secretary to prepare a National Curriculum that would make explicit the goals pupils were to pursue, the curriculum followed and the learning levels that had been achieved against national targets. Parents would be able to judge their children's progress against agreed national targets for attainment and would also be able to judge the effectiveness of their schools. One of the leading administrators of the legislation, N. Stuart, set out clearly the objectives of the Education Reform Act in a public lecture to the 18th BEMAS Annual Conference in 1989:

> (i) above all, *to raise standards of attainment for all pupils* by a better definition of what is to be taught and learnt; the greater involvement of a better-informed parent body; and greater autonomy and hence responsibility for individual schools in the way in which they deploy all their resources to this end;

> (ii) what is thus involved is to increase substantially public information available to parents about what pupils are to be taught; what they have achieved; what the resources of the school are; and how the school deploys them. *Better accountability applied to more informed parental choice*, which various aspects of the Act seek to enlarge;

> (iii) to improve the overall management of the service by delegating decision-making as close as possible to the point where the decisions bite. *Better management* and a better curriculum go hand in hand.

The Education Reform Act strove to realize these objectives with two principal strategies. The first was to establish more rigorous planning of teaching and learning throughout the system. The creation of a National Curriculum would provide an entitlement to broad and balanced learning for all 5–16-year-olds, while achievement would be assessed by a range of assessment procedures. Such close monitoring of progress in learning would enable parents to know more clearly what was being studied, what objectives were being set and what was being achieved individually and collectively. This kind of information would provide the basis of the second principal strategy, of increasing the accountability of the service to parents and the public generally.

The National Curriculum was criticized from the first for possessing too restricted a view of the core and foundation subjects (Walton, 1988; Ouseley, 1988) and for imposing a repressive regime of assessment tests at 7, 11, 14 and 16. As Murphy (1988) explained, such tests would limit the progression in learning that the National Curriculum purported to encourage.

Thus the working of the market place was not to be left entirely to the hidden hand of competitive self-interest. Rather it was to be intepreted and guided by the 'public' hand of the Secretary of State, who would be granted an extraordinary new range of regulatory powers that would more reflect Bentham's panopticon than Nozick's minimal state. The market would be monitored by ministers. Schools might be 'privatized' progressively but their reproduction of culture (the curriculum) would be nationalized (or anglicized). (The pamphlet from Hillgate clearly had been more influential than that from the Adam Smith Institute or the IEA: see Jones (1989) on the tensions between the traditionalists and the marketeers in the new right.)

Between the emerging forces of the market and Whitehall hierarchy it appeared that the centre-piece of the 1944 legislation – the local education authority and the local government of education – had been considerably reduced in authority: its former powers were dissolved or redistributed. The way the education profession often liked to describe the governance of education in the post-war years – as a national service locally administered – was mistaken then but seemed to becoming a reality.

Marginalizing the LEA: 1991

The government of education, having been recast by the 1988 Education Reform Act, once more became the focus of radical change, with significant consequences for the public domain. The local education authority, at the centre of the earlier reforms, was again in the eye of the storm as the purported cause of the service's continuing problems. Although the 1988 Education Reform Act redefined responsibilities and withdrew powers from the LEA, it nevertheless accorded it, potentially, a leading role in the implementation of the reforms to local management and of the National Curriculum. The challenge for the new LEA was to set aside its traditional commitment to controlling the routine administration of local education and to concentrate instead on clarifying strategy and assuring quality. A providing authority was to give way to an enabling authority. Many LEAs, although developing different perspectives on the new local management of education, clearly committed themselves to the task of reform (Ranson, 1992a) and, moreover, it became possible to indicate achievements that enhanced the objectives of the 1988 reforms.

By 1991 the very conception of education government embodied in that legislation – of a strategic LEA leading an integrated though devolved system of institutional governance – was giving way to a very different vision of independent institutions supported, at most, by a 'service agency' LEA. In March, the Secretary of State, Mr Clarke, in a radio broadcast asserted that the natural progression for schools would be to move out of the LEA system, with the LEA focusing on residual (special) needs; and in May, the Prime Minister argued for the need to break up 'the monolith' of the local education system (while a senior civil servant, later in the year, alluded metaphorically to 'ploughing the ground'). Ministerial speeches and announcements routinely appeared to criticize the LEA.

The 1988 reforms of the local system of governance were being quietly but radically revised: any vestigial authority of the LEA was being increasingly eroded, but piecemeal and without public debate of the entire scheme. The 1988 legislation, despite the limitations of public consultation, was nevertheless of a piece and brought to Parliament whole: now the parts were brought into view in dribs and drabs. The effect of this process, in both the manner and the substance of the changes, was to generate considerable instability for the local system of education in a way that was likely to undermine the quality of learning for many within schools and colleges. This period saw initiatives that would significantly alter the 1988 system of government: in particular, the encouragement of opting out, and the proposed legislation on further education and schools.

Self-governing schools

Ministerial statements on *opting out* had risen in intensity over the months from January 1991, when Mr Clarke told the North of England Education Conference that he wanted to secure the 'positive growth' of the GM sector; in February, he admitted for the first time that GM schools were receiving more resources than LEA schools and he speculated that in time the differential would narrow. Press reports in March cited a leaked Conservative Party document expecting that nearly all schools would have opted out within five years, a story confirmed by the Secretary of State in a television interview in March in which he revealed: 'It remains my view that, particularly for the secondary sector, GM status should become a norm, not an exception.'

By November 1991:

- 135 schools had been approved for GM status (102 were operating as such);
- 236 schools (out of 26,000 in England and Wales: until 1990 only 6,700 schools were eligible to opt out) had formally voted in favour, had published proposals, had had proposals approved or were then operating as GM schools; of these
  46 were primary schools
  167 were county council schools
  47 were London (outer/inner) schools
  155 were in Conservative councils (65.7 per cent)
  49 were in Labour councils (20.8 per cent)
  32 were in hung councils (13.6 per cent).

The movement to grant-maintained status had been slow, although in parts of the country it began to accelerate. The causes were various: 19 per cent of the 236 schools had been the subject of reorganization proposals, some saw the potential to restore, in time, their former grammar school status and there was evidence of a relationship between opting out and low spending by LEAs (Rogers, 1991; Ranson, 1992a). The response of the Government to the slow progress of one of its leading policies had been to introduce a number of incentives for wavering schools. For example, there were increases in start-up grants for GM schools and the prospect of substantial capital grants. Then, in April, Mr Clarke announced that he was easing the informal temporary interdiction on change of character of a GM school (e.g. that it could now apply to become a grammar school, or to develop a sixth form, without having first to run for five years as a GM school). One of the most significant changes was an innocuous-looking proposal by the DES, out of administrative convenience, to set at 16 per cent of its annual maintenance grant the amount of cash a GM school might get from its formerly maintaining LEA. This suggestion, which Ministers adopted and subsequently modified in the light of the Association of County Councils' consultants' evidence, was highly controversial, especially to LEAs that had already delegated disproportionately large amounts of their general schools budgets (GSB) under schemes of local management (LMS); if the GM school were to get not only the large pupil-related budget that it would have received as an LEA school under LMS, but also 16 per cent of the basic grant as well, the incentive to opt out would be all the greater. This measure had the most serious and immediate consequences for many LEAs. A study commissioned from Coopers & Lybrand Deloitte by the Association of County Councils (ACC) demonstrated how an authority would not be able to afford its central administration at a projected stage to be determined by whether it was mainly primary or mainly secondary schools that were leaving (and, especially in the case of secondaries, what their sizes were). Research indicated that some LEAs had already begun to face up to the prospect of administrative non-viability: more than 40 per cent of the secondary schools had opted out in Ealing, Hillingdon and Bromley while in Hertfordshire the figure was 22 per cent and in Kent 19 per cent.

The incentives to opt out were complemented by the policies to reinforce competition between schools expressed in DES Circular 7/91 of 23 April on local management of schools. The Circular sought to strengthen the principles of LMS by increasing the delegation of resources, increasing pupil-led funding (which Thomas (1988) had termed the voucher element of LMS) and providing for the extension of delegated management to all primary schools, as well as accelerating delegation to any school. These policies would weaken the capacity of LEAs to use what limited capacity they originally had to distribute recourses according to need and would encourage schools to accumulate more pupils to expand their resources. LMS, as it was formulated, was not a neutral system of management: its principles sought to constitute competition between schools.

LMS within the LEA was now clearly conceived as a staging post towards GM status and independence from the LEA. The further and higher education legislation achieved independence for colleges by a different route. The rapid transition from the Education Reform Act's prescription of local management of colleges, with the single and probably misplaced subsection allowing for incorporation by mutual agreement and ministerial permission, to universal incorporation and detachment from the LEA exemplifies shifts in policy and the instability of the 1988 legislation.

Incorporation of colleges

The financial necessity for the Government to remove the burden of £2 billion of expenditure permanently from local revenue made FE a target for change. In the context of financial statements on 21 March 1991, the Secretary of State foretold of a White Paper on the creation of funding councils for further education in England and Wales, to finance colleges, which would be given corporate status. The White Paper was launched in May by the Prime Minister, who promised a major programme of reform of post-compulsory education and training for the twenty-first century. Its primary objectives were: to ensure that virtually the whole of the 16–19 age group were drawn into education and training; to reform post-16 qualifications; to raise the status of vocational studies; and to provide employers with a dominating voice within the new system. A new 16–18 college sector of education was in effect being proposed. From 1 April 1993, colleges of further education together with tertiary and sixth form colleges would be given independent corporate status and would form a directly funded sector focusing upon the needs of over two million full- and part-time students.

With charitable status funded through two councils, one each for England and Wales, and advised, in England, by seven to ten regional advisory committees with offices and staff, these new councils, with strong industrial, commercial and professional represen- tation, would be appointed by the Education Secretary in consultation with the Employ- ment Secretary. They would have wide-ranging powers and responsibilities for the new sector, including the planning of provision, incorporation of the power to determine what kind of courses colleges should offer, control of the allocation of annual funding as well as capital resources, and the duty to monitor the quality of college performance.

The LEAs would have only a tenuous link with the new college sector, being asked merely to *liaise* with the colleges, while local councillors would only be able to serve on the governing bodies of the colleges if invited to do so. The Government, some inter- preted, was 'determined to ensure a complete rupture between the colleges and their present masters' (*TES*, 24 May 1991, p. 4). Members of the Training and Enterprise Councils, however, were to be accorded the right to become governors.

> After the reforms instruments of government will no longer provide for formal LEA representation. The legislation will, however, remove the provision in the 1988 Education Reform Act which prevents people who are local authority members or employees from being co-opted on to governing bodies. Governing bodies will be able to co-opt two addi- tional members. This means that some governors may well combine their public service on the governing body with membership of a local authority. They will be co-opted for their individual qualities, and not as delegates or representatives of the local authority. . . . Existing employment interest governors should be supplemented by a representative of a local TEC. This will reflect the TECs' important contribution to training locally and their increasing involvement in vocational education.
>
> (DES, 1991, vol. 2, p. 21)

The colleges would be funded in part from an Education and Training Council grant. This would comprise two components: a cash-limited block grant, and a further amount based upon student admissions. Colleges would continue to derive funds from: TEC grants under the work-related further education programme; grants from polytechnics if they undertook some higher education work; fee income from employers and students; and consultancy and other services. The colleges would be able to offer training credits, which were vouchers for 16- or 17-year-olds to pay for part-time vocational education and training. The scheme would be managed by the TECs, and was piloted in 11 areas of the country. The White Paper proposed that by 1996 all 16- or 17-year-olds would be offered training credits to pay for vocational education and training.

This wide-ranging reconstituting of the governance of post-16 education and training was designed to support reforms that would ostensibly break down the divide between academic and vocational systems of learning and qualification. A vocationally oriented competence-based curriculum and assessment was to be given parity of esteem with the academic:

Young people and adults need a clear framework of qualifications to measure their success in education and training. We need to build up a modern system of academic and vocational qualifications which are equally valued. They must both set a high standard and offer ladders of opportunity after sixteen and throughout working life. . . . Vocational qualifications in this country have been undervalued and underused. A major reform is under way to produce clear, nationally recognised qualifications. The reform is led by the National Council for Vocational Qualifications . . . the NCVQ should work with others to develop criteria for accrediting more vocational qualifications.

(DES, 1991, vol. 1, p. 16)

At the same time, a framework of principles would be designed to ensure the quality of all A level and AS syllabuses. New diplomas would encompass these academic (e.g. A levels) and vocational (NVQ) qualifications. The Government intended that these principles should control the development of syllabuses, limiting assessment by coursework and establishing examinations at the end of courses as the norm. Other changes included:

- school sixth forms to be allowed to admit part-time and adult students, and to accept training credits or to charge fees for them;
- education compacts to be extended nationwide (these are bargains between young people, employers and colleges – young people work towards personal goals and in return employers provide a job with training for those who achieve their goals);
- vocational adult education to be funded through colleges and leisure/social adult education to be funded by fees.

Local authorities and the teacher associations had been critical of the implications of the White Paper for: first, the development of coherent strategies and plans for the post-compulsory education and training which had been at the centre of the 1988 Education Reform Act; second, the narrow, utilitarian conception of the purposes of education and training; third, special educational needs post-16. The influence of the TECs and a tendency to output measurement of performance were already leaving students and trainees with special educational needs at the margin. The *Times Educational Supplement* concluded that 'even if reducing local taxation is no longer an electoral imperative, the government is going out of its way to strip the local authorities of responsibility or influence in further education and its support services' (24 May 1991, p. 4).

The Further and Higher Education Bill was presented to Parliament in early November 1991. This legislation anticipated the dismantling of the binary system of higher education, creating a single structure for universities, polytechnics and colleges of higher education under one funding council. The possibility of polytechnics taking up, if they wished, the title of university might have suggested the expansion and comprehensivization of higher education to accommodate an increase of 30 per cent in the participation rate. But the indications from the DFE and the Universities Funding Council (UFC) that a small number of universities (perhaps ten) were to specialize in research were confirmed in Mr Clarke's December announcement of the inevitable emergence of a research university super-league.

The power of inspection

The most significant indication of a shift in policy was provided by the announcement – again a gradual revelation – that LEAs would lose the statutory power of inspecting and assuring the quality of their own schools, increasing fears that the role of the LEA established by the 1988 ERA was being rapidly diminished.[1] The gradualness was shown in the sequence: first, Her Majesty's Senior Chief Inspector (SCI) announced his early retirement; then the job was advertised; the Secretary of State then called for a departmental review of HMI, cancelled the appointment process for the post and designated a senior member of the Inspectorate as SCI *pro tempore*. *The Citizen's Charter* White Paper was meanwhile followed by *The Parent's Charter*, proposing the publication of 'league tables' of examination results, and outlining substantial changes in arrangements for school inspections. Ministerial conclusions after the HMI review were promptly enshrined in the Education (Schools) Bill 1991, presented in the same week as the FHE Bill. LEAs expressed a range of views, most of them critical, about the new role proposed for HMI, largely to preside over a system of registered inspectors, who could tender for school inspections to be commissioned by governing bodies. But the focal point of LEA concern was the proposed repeal of s. 77 (3) of the Education Act 1944 (the LEA's powers to inspect), together with the requirement that, if LEA inspectors were to inspect schools, they would have to tender successfully for the job.

Consultations on these proposals ended some ten days *after* the Bill had been given its first reading. The second reading debate, on 19 November, produced no soothing words for LEAs, whose inspectors were condemned in, among other passages, the Secretary of State's quotation of an eightfold critique by the Secondary Heads Association. Mr Clarke also made some more generalized attacks on authorities' stewardship of educational standards. Again doubt fell on the 1988 dispensations. The LEAs curricular responsibilities had been reasonably clearly set out in Sir Keith Joseph's No. 2 Act of 1986, but restricted by Mr Kenneth Baker's Act of 1988, with more prominence given to the roles of governing body and headteacher and, of course, the prescriptions of the National Curriculum. But the assertion of DES Circular 7/88 that LMS was about quality of schooling reflected at least the implications of the 1988 Act that the LEA was crucially responsible for monitoring and evaluating its schools, with the outcomes of such monitoring informing the continuing processes of budget setting and oversight of LMS.

Removal of the power to inspect, underlined by transfer of resources for inspection to schools to fund the new contractors, appeared to cut right across the evaluatory function of the LEA. If s. 77 (3) were to go, then most of the legal justifications for the LEA's continuation as schools authority depended on the enabling powers of s. 111 of the Local Government Act 1972, and what might be inferred from such duties as those of the employer, maintainer of the structures of buildings, overseer of teacher appraisal, and budget spender of last resort. How to discharge the 1944 Act's duty to secure efficient education (s. 7) in sufficient and adequately equipped schools (s. 8) suddenly looked problematic. The only area where it seemed that LEAs and ministers were at one was the centrality of the LEA in ensuring special educational provision for children with special needs.

Suspicions had been growing in the early part of the year that Mr Clarke was not attached to the Teachers' Pay and Conditions Bill inherited from his predecessor. Confirmation came with the presentation of a new Bill, replacing limited collective bargaining with a review body, unique in covering staff who were not employed nationally and other conditions of service than pay. The Bill was enacted.

During 1991, therefore, the Government embarked on a programme of change that implied a fundamental revision of the conception of the government of education embodied in its own radical 1988 Education Reform Act. While senior civil servants in public conferences acknowledged that it would take a decade for those reforms to be fully implemented and evaluated, now it appeared that the Government had already pre-judged one of its key innovations as a failure. The LEA was undoubtedly beleaguered: its expenditure often capped or contracted, schools increasingly induced to leave, colleges about to be appropriated and, finally, the principal responsibility accorded it in the 1988 reforms now to be put into the market place. Throughout, the LEA's contribution was denigrated and ridiculed by Ministers.

The LEA, charged in 1988 with the task of providing local schools and colleges with strategic leadership and assuring the quality of local education, was now in the process of being diminished to a service agency role or, if the political committee of the Conservative Carlton Club had its way, to be eliminated in favour of regional boards. Either eventuality would mean the end of the local government of education. It became clear that the most significant questions facing the service surrounded the necessity for an LEA: this is more important than the controversy of testing or the National Curriculum, because the questions involved the nature of our democracy, what constitutes effective management of institutions, and what the preconditions are for achievement by young people in classrooms. From 1991 the legislative proposals made clear the Government's answers – so that the future of the local government of education (even of the kind envisaged in 1988) seemed in considerable doubt.

The 1993 Education Act: the demise of the local government of education

The 1993 Education Act marks a further and decisive phase in the Conservative Government's reform movement, which has taken a decisive turn to deconstruct local *systems* of education. Under the mask of continuing the changes begun in 1988, the 1992 White Paper *Choice and Diversity* in fact marked a final break with the post-war values of universalism in favour of an earlier tradition, never eliminated, of private and selective education. At the centre of this quiet revolution lies an attack upon the public and democratic foundations of education and upon the equal opportunities they strive to constitute.

Although there is the semblance of continuity between 1988 and 1992 there is actually a fundamental shift of policy. In place of 'progression', 'entitlement' and 'local management' is substituted a new emphasis upon 'standards', 'specialization', 'selection' and 'autonomy' (see Table 5.1). The elements of the new paradigm will be discussed in turn.

Standards

In the autumn of 1991 Lord Griffiths (the new head of SEAC) had unveiled a more 'streamlined' package of tests for 7-year-olds. The first national tests for this group had been taken during the summer and reviewed, and the results were announced in September. The Government concluded that the tests took too long and were unmanageable. In future tests would be simpler, with 'a sharper focus on the basics'. Teachers and advisers became increasingly concerned, however, that such announcements (including

Table 5.1. *From 1988 to 1993*

	1988	1993
Mission	Public choice and accountability (entitlement)	Choice and diversity (differentiation)
Learning process	An entitlement curriculum, progression, assessment	Specialization, standards, testing
Institutional system	Local delegation (LMS)	School autonomy (GM), college incorporation
Government	National education, locally administered	Nationalization of education
	The enabling LEA	Demise of the LEA, especially the role of local democracy
		Regional funding agencies
	Governing body	Foundation governors
	Parental choice	Parental power
	Quality assurance/development	Quality control/inspections
Context	Economic crisis	Economic and social crises

the reduction of course work in GCSE) accorded greater value to the content than the process of learning (for example, investigation in science, or the experience of drafting in English). If in future the standard attainment targets (SATs) would not fully assess the full range of the prescribed programmes of study the question was raised as to how long the elaborate requirements of the National Curriculum would survive.

Launching the 1992 White Paper, the Prime Minister (John Major) said that 'the drive for higher standards in schools has been the hallmark of the Government over the last decade' and is now to be carried forward. Testing is to be the key to monitoring and raising standards in schools. From 1992 a different conception of learning within the National Curriculum began to emerge: a move away from an emphasis upon progression in understanding, skills and capacity, taking into account the needs of the child as a whole person as well as the requirements of learning through the National Curriculum. The move towards a basic standards model of the curriculum entrenches even more securely than the subject-based National Curriculum a conception of learning as the inculcation of disaggregated bodies of knowledge, a 'collection code' curriculum, and of assessment as the sorting and differentiating of young people. It reinforces a notion of fixed levels of ability, the 'normal curve' of achievement and different 'types' of aptitude and ability.

Specialization

Diversity and parental choice are celebrated to 'allow schools to develop in different ways. In particular they encourage schools to play to their strengths. Some schools stress an all ability curriculum; others in addition to the National Curriculum specialise in one or a small number of subjects' (DFE, 1992, p. 9). Diversity offers parents and children greater choice: private and state schools, county and voluntary; comprehensive schools of variety, grammar and bilateral; CTCs and grant-maintained schools. Some schools will choose to specialize in music or technology or languages. Diversity, it is proposed, extinguishes the anathema of uniformity, which 'in educational provision presupposes that all children have basically the same educational needs. The reality is that children have different needs. The provision of education should be geared more to local circumstances and individual needs: hence our commitment to diversity in education' (DFE, 1992, p. 3).

This discussion implies that specialization might proceed beyond different emphases of subject into different types of learning and school: academic, technological and creative. These distinctions recall the terms of tripartite education – grammar, technical and modern – outlined in the 1938 Spens Report and the 1943 Norwood Report and introduced into the secondary system after the Second World War. Indeed, the 1992 White Paper refers affectionately to this tripartite system of secondary schools, which, it implies, would have proved an ideal education system if it had only been supported by a national curriculum to provide equality of opportunity! Like the 1940s Reports, the 1992 White Paper expresses its commitment to 'parity of esteem' between different types of school. It is argued that schools can develop such specialization 'within existing powers': 'it generally does not constitute a significant change of character requiring the approval of the Secretary of State. If schools wish to develop in this way responding to the aspirations of parents and local economic needs, then it is entirely appropriate that they should use the discretion vested in them to do so.'

Selection

The possibility that specialization or differentiation might entail selection is denied: 'Specialisation is often confused with selection . . . A school that specialises is not necessarily one that applies rigid academic criteria for entry, for a non-selective school can also choose to specialise.' Yet the word 'selection' appears in a title of prescribed values together with 'specialization' and 'standards', and the White Paper acknowledges that selection *could* take place through parental choice: 'as schools develop their strengths, they may become more attractive to parents and pupils. The greater demand to attend the school the greater the resources that will flow to the school . . . the selection that takes place is parent driven.'

Institutional autonomy

While the 1988 Education Reform Act introduced the possibility of schools 'opting out' into grant-maintained status it is a contested issue whether the originating conception for GM schools was as the future of all schools, or as a privileged sector like the old 'direct grant' schools, or as an exception (for schools seeking to escape purported 'undesirable LEAs'!). The norm was, arguably, intended to be 'locally managed schools' within an LEA but with considerable discretion over the use of resources within local strategic policy planning. Yet since 1991 ministers have been promoting a very different policy that 'GM status should become a norm not an exception'. Institutional autonomy rather than discretion has now become the key value of government.

The demise of the LEA

The introduction of a new Funding Agency for Schools (FAS), controlled from Whitehall, is to be introduced to control finance but also to rationalize institutions. As opting out accelerates, the FAS is conceived as replacing the LEA in relation to primary and secondary schools. Any obstacles that might resist an increase in the 'organizational flexibility' of the LEA in the evolution of its residual functions will be removed, 'in particular the requirement to establish an Education Committee. Some local authorities may soon be in sight of no longer needing them.' As the Bill passed through Parliament and amendment to s. 1 of the 1944 Education Act removed any reference to the local education authority!

Thus the emphases of the 1992 and 1993 legislative changes mark a significant change for the government of education. They establish a new consistency of governance to replace the contradictions of entitlement and choice. Now the principles of student differentiation and selection sit harmoniously with the established policy of institutional differentiation. The changes, by reinforcing market forces, are likely to entrench the reintroduction of tripartite education.

Perhaps the defining characteristic of the present restructuring of the government of education is the attack upon its local democratic foundations. Its attempt to remove education (schools and colleges) from local politics presents the most significant indication of the termination of the post-war social democratic era in which local government played the pivotal role in the development of public services for all. The de-democratizing of local education is not a peripheral element: it is, arguably, its central purpose. At this stage, an American study that has been influential with the Government (a civil servant indicated that Ministers had made it prescribed reading) needs to be critically analysed.

Markets versus democracy in education

Chubb and Moe, in their *Politics, Markets and America's Schools* (1990) (popularized in the *Sunday Times* magazine in February 1992), seek to argue that local democracy is the source of the problem of failing schools. This argument proceeds through a number of stages. The presenting problem is that schools are failing in their core academic mission: maths, science, foreign languages, etc. Children are not learning enough, or the right things, or learning how to learn.

Two waves of reforms designed to remedy this situation have helped only marginally. The first wave of reforms introduced tighter standards for teacher certification, higher teacher salaries, career ladders, merit pay, stricter disciplinary policy, more homework and standardized tests. The second wave of reform, looking remarkably like our own 1988 reforms, encouraged school-based management, teacher professionalism and controlled choice for parents and pupils. These reforms, though contributing a little, were deemed to be failing because they were not identifying and addressing the underlying cause. The reforms were therefore destined to fail. The task was to develop a theory that explained failure. Such a theory was to be found in institutional analysis. Because schools are shaped by their institutional settings, the kinds of organization they become are largely a reflection of the institutional contexts in which they operate.

While the reformers believed that the source of the problems lay in and around schools, that schools could be made better within existing contexts, Chubb and Moe argue that existing institutions cannot solve the problem because they *are* the problem. The very institutions that are supposed to solve the problem are the source of the problem – that is, institutions of direct democratic control. These institutions, Chubb and Moe believe, are incompatible with effective schooling: direct democratic control undermines academic performance.

The institutional characteristics of the public sector, it is argued, create problems for schools. The game of local democracy constitutes a perpetual struggle for power that creates winners and losers. This makes democracy an essentially coercive institution: the winners impose their policies at the expense of the others. The *raison d'être* of democracy is for the winners to impose their higher-order values, which they realize through rules and procedures. Bureaucratic and hierarchical control, therefore, arises naturally and inevitably out of this process of democracy because of the need to ensure compliance.

Schools are trapped within these institutional arrangements. They cannot set their own agendas because these are determined by politicians and administrators, who impose their values upon schools: for example, 'sex education', 'socialization of immigrants', 'the mainstreaming of the handicapped', 'bilingual education' or 'what history to teach'. The ensuing paraphernalia of rules stifles the autonomy of schools and demotivates the teachers. Institutions work when people choose them. The key to better schools thus lies in institutional reform, which reinforces choice and therefore commitment. The appropriate institutional setting for education lies in (or in some semblance of) the private sector, in which:

- society controls schools through the market rather than democratic politics;
- authority is radically decentralized, enabling discretion and promoting autonomy;
- no one makes decisions for society;
- all participants make decisions for themselves;
- markets are myopic, offering what people want through selection and sorting;
- organizations and consumers are matched;
- to be successful schools need to find a niche, a specialized segment of the market to which they can appeal and attract support (the obvious way to do this is through the strategic design of their curricula, targeting particular values, such as discipline, religion, socio-economic and ethnic make-up of students);
- the market allows and encourages its schools to have distinctive, well-defined 'missions'.

Although markets have imperfections, it is argued that they are preferable to those of public authority: democratic control tends to promote bureaucracy, while markets tend to promote autonomy. Thus, according to Chubb and Moe, the institutional conditions for effective schools are the de-democratization of institutional setting and the creation of a market setting, which constitutes decentralization, competition, choice autonomy, clarity of mission, strong leadership, teacher professionalism and team cooperation.

THE MACHINERY OF THE MARKET: A CRITIQUE

The Conservative Government has over time introduced complex administrative regulations that are designed to create a highly structured market of educational choice. It can be argued, however, that while appearing to liberate consumers the market in fact entrenches most in a deeper and less accountable structure of control. The market institutionalizes rules and relationships which develop with inexorable force to erode local democracy and to reinforce a segmented social structure.

In this section an interpretive analysis of the organizing principles of an education market is developed (it builds upon Dworkin, 1985; Sen, 1985, 1990; Ranson, 1988; Jonathan, 1990; Whitty, 1989; Levacic, 1991; Miliband, 1991; Ball, 1990a, b, 1992a, b; Bowe *et al.*, 1992; Edwards and Whitty, 1992; Elster, 1992). The layered workings of the market are examined in turn: its conception of possessive individuals; the institutionalizing of instrumental rationality; the commodification of education; the reinforcing of a class-divided society; and a polity increasingly bereft of democracy. This discussion will suggest that the market is flawed in conception as a vehicle for improving educational opportunities: it can only radically contract them.

An atrophied psychology of possessive individualism

The organizing principles of the market order make assumptions about the public, about their orientation, capacities and resources. When individuals pursue their own interests, it is claimed, they will benefit society as much as themselves: 'I have never known much good done by those who affected to trade for the public good' (Adam Smith). However, the conception of the public as only self-interested consumers ('possessive individuals'; Macpherson, 1973) presents a degraded and distorted psychology of human nature. Not only does it clearly mistake the diversity of qualities that inform individual motivation (making unintelligible Titmuss's (1971) illustration of blood donation as the paradigm of civic virtue), conflating individual purpose with self-interest furthermore misconstrues the nature of individuality itself. It assumes that my purposes, my development, must always be at the expense of someone else's. It makes every interaction and relationship a 'zero-sum' game: my success depends upon your defeat. An alternative vision of individuality can not only acknowledge the separateness and distinctiveness of each but also perceive them as enriching rather than diminishing others. Indeed, others are indispensable to the unfolding of the self: my capacities require your support while your identity warrants my recognition. The Athenian world of Pericles valued the separateness of each person as a fundamental ethical value and the importance of private liberty, but celebrated, too, citizens' membership of and responsibility towards their community. Individuals were autonomous *and* interdependent. This is, of course, the significant duality of citizenship – of an individual-as-a-member-of-the-community.

The point is not that individuals are by nature possessively self-interested, but that the institutions of the market require that orientation as the only appropriate disposition. Individuals are not intrinsically selfish but markets make them so. The institution of the market demands a singular currency of transaction. In this sense the market is ill-suited to social as against economic relationships because it simplifies human beings and denies the complexity of their individuality and interdependence.

The institutionalizing of instrumental rationality

Some of the most important writing in the human sciences is preoccupied with the unintended public consequences of private decision-making: with the growing realization, especially in many public services, that self-interest can be self-defeating. Competitive individualism in the education market reproduces this paradox, with a difference: while it holds true for most, some are more than likely to make self-interest self-succeeding.

The market normally assumes that all goods and services are discrete, unchanging, products. If I purchase a chocolate bar my purchase has no effect on the product although pressure may be placed upon production or delivery. But in education, the market has chameleon-like qualities that can actually change the characteristics of the goods being purchased. My preference for a school, privately expressed, together with the unwitting choices of others, can transform the product. A small school grows in scale, with inevitable consequences for learning style and administrative process. The distinctive ethos that was the reason for the choice may be altered by the choice.

These seemingly unpredictable collective outcomes of private choice can create for any individual the disturbing effect of bringing into question the very rationality of action in the education market place. Rational agency implies that an actor is able to calculate the means necessary to realize defined purposes. The actor is able to formulate intentions *ex ante* with the reasonable expectation that preferences can, other things being equal, translate into actions. But in markets like education 'things' are not equal. The unintended consequences of multiple and independent transactions leave any and every actor completely in the dark about what it is rational to believe is being chosen. Outcomes are, in principle, chronically unpredicatable, literally out of anybody's control. This anarchic quality of markets is one of the characteristics that critics emphasize. Markets can thus appear to be beyond rational decision and influence.

This leaves actors having to base their actions on extrinsic considerations, on judgements about the context they are in or the outcome of others' transactions, rather than considerations that are internal to their own value-informed purposes. The actor is continually constrained to react, to judge *ex post* what it is best to do. For example, a number of schools have not wished to opt out, disagreeing with the assumptions on which that policy is based. Yet a moment can arrive when the governors and the head feel constrained to judge, in a context of changing admissions and resources, that if the interests of the institution (in survival) are clarified then a conclusion to opt out is inescapable.

This begins to illustrate the underlying rationality of market transactions. If exchange drives out value-based purposive action, it nevertheless reinforces instrumental rationality. Action in the market is driven in upon a single common currency: the pursuit of material interests. The only effective means upon which to base action is the calculation of personal advantage: clout in the market derives from the power of superior resources to subordinate others in competitive exchange.

The paradox of consumer choice empowering the producers

The rhetoric in market theory is that in competitive exchange consumers are 'sovereign', and that producers will adapt their commodities to suit the changing preferences of consumers while, in the face of competition, reducing costs to remain efficient. The influence of consumers ostensibly makes producers endlessly responsive. However, a more realistic assessment of the working of markets would acknowledge the tendency of exchange to empower producers at the expense of increasingly dependent consumers.

This happens in education because parental choice presupposes a significant margin of surplus school capacity. But the markets work as their designers might have intended: some schools fill to overcapacity while others dwindle, are forced to close and thus remove from the system those places required to enable choice. Schools then begin to choose and enter into competition to select particular parents: those with high-performing children and those with surplus resources to support the educational needs of the institution.

The evidence thus grows in education as much as in other markets that producers select consumers or, more subtly, some producers and consumers search each other out in a progressive segmentation of the market. Schools begin to differentiate themselves to fit specific niches in the educational market, perhaps as an 'academic' school or a 'technology' school. The institutions begin to market what they believe to be their distinctive image, qualities and achievements. A hierarchy of distinction and public esteem emerges: 'different categories of schools will attempt to differentiate themselves by what they offer beyond the National Curriculum, and a hierarchy of status will emerge, backed by additional funding from parents and industry and differential selection policies' (Tomlinson, 1988).

The paradox of choice reducing choice

It is likely in an education market, therefore, that the intention of increasing choice results not only in the product being altered but also in choice itself being reduced or eliminated. This paradox does not emerge by chance but from the principles that emerge to govern interaction in the market. The search by each individual to advance his or her interests in competition with others causes those who win to secure their relative advantage by restricting supply, or scope of access to privileged goods and resources. This results in a hierarchy of esteem that reduces choice for many to a contracting good (see Echols *et al*. (1990) on Scotland, where choice leads to re-elevation of the traditionally privileged schools).

The commodification of education

When education is regarded as an unfolding learning process that can be adapted continuously to suit the needs of particular individuals then it is neither a commodity nor a process that is appropriate to the market place. The changing needs of individuals, given these purposes, cannot be packaged and marketed; nor can the institution that is a vehicle for their realization, because it is changed and damaged by the market.

Nevertheless, these intrinsic processes of learning, when located in market settings, are turned into packageable products whose acquisition may confer privileged social status.

This preoccupation with the search for distinction accentuates competition, which turns education into what Hirsch (1977; see also Miliband, 1991) calls a 'positional good'. Because education is an institution that society can use to 'screen' or 'filter' individuals into privileged occupations, competition intensifies as individuals aspire to acquire qualifications with the highest exchange value. Education, like original works of art, or a house by the sea, can become a 'positional good', something by definition in scarce supply. Where the good, like education, is subject to congestion or crowding it is relative advantage that each strives for, necessarily at the expense of others:

> Since education has exchange value as well as intrinsic value, and since its value in exchange like that of any other currency depends not on the amount of this good that an individual holds in absolute terms, but rather the amount she holds *relative to others*, then a more favourable experience – in exchange value terms – secured for one child, entails a less favourable experience in those terms for some other child or children.
>
> (Jonathan, 1990)

When competition intensifies for positional goods with limited supply their price rises relative to other goods.

> The rise in the price of positional goods will choke off any excess demand for such goods. To that extent there is 'pure' social scarcity, in that satisfaction is derived from scarcity itself, the price mechanism is the basic regulator containing demand within the limits of inherently restricted supply. Allocation proceeds in effect, through the auction of a restricted set of objects to the highest bidder.
>
> (Hirsch, 1977, p. 28)

This spiralling process of positional competition, with individuals and institutions striving for relative advantage, leads, as Jonathan perceptively argues, to pressures that conserve the type of education that dominates the status hierarchy:

> Thus deregulation in the distribution of education increases the climate of competition for access to whatever form of it has highest exchange value, and individuals who seek to maximise the exchange value of their or their children's experience must underwrite whatever cognitive skills and social attitudes are at a premium in the evolving cultural ethos.
>
> (Jonathan, 1990)

Because consumers cannot change the structure of the market but only protect or advance their position relative to others within the existing status order, their self-interested actions serve only to reproduce forms of education of which they may well not approve.

The currency of this conforming commodity market is thus unmistakably social status: the search on the part of schools and parents to enter into the mutual creation of an exclusive institution. The price paid by consumers for entry into privileged market niches is manifestation of cultural capital: ownership of distinctive capacities, resources, power and influence. The educational market becomes the social manifestation of Darwinian natural selection. Species of institutions survive according to their capacity to discover and adapt to their distinctive social environments: that is, social class settings.

Reinforcing a class-divided society

The assumption that all parents and their communities actually behave as possessive consumers is the new ideology of 'parentocracy' (Brown, 1990), promoting the values of calculative choosing as the defining quality of ideal parenting appropriate to the market. The good parents are good choosers. But, as Ball and co-workers argue, this neglects significant variations in cultural dispositions of classes and minority ethnic communities:

> The system of choice presupposes sets of values which give primacy to comparison, mobility and long term planning, it ignores those cultures which give primacy to the values of community and locality. The social and geographical horizons of stable communities may be limited and the proximity and the history of the local school may be valued in their own right.
>
> (Bowe *et al.*, 1992)

The practice of choice depends upon 'cultural capital', that knowledge, underpinned by dispositions, skills and capacities, which, accumulated over time by the middle classes, lends them significant advantages in market transactions:

> The role of cultural capital in relation to choice is both general and specific. General, in the sense that certain types and amounts of cultural capital are required to be an active and strategic chooser. For example, knowledge of local schools, access to and ability to read and decipher significant information, ability to engage with and decipher the 'promotional' activities of schools (like open evenings, brochures and videos), the ability to maximise choice by 'working the system' (making multiple applications, applying for scholarships etc.), and the ability to engage in activities involving positive presentation of self (e.g. when meeting key gatekeepers). Specific, in the sense that the making of 'successful' choices, getting your first choice, can depend upon direct engagement and advocacy and pursuit of your choice. There are points of articulation in the choice process when certain kinds of cultural capital are crucial. For example, in the case of oversubscribed schools, the capacity to make direct approaches to the school or to follow the legalistic process of 'Appeal' (mounting an effective case). . . . An inability or unwillingness to participate in these aspects of 'choosing' or an ignorance of them among certain class groups is what Bourdieu and Passeron call 'self-exclusion' based in part perhaps upon a belief that the system does not work for them.
>
> (Ball, 1992a, p. 11)

The capital required to exercise the dispositions of possessive individualism is material as well as cultural. It is assumed that all parents have the resources available to them to facilitate choosing and to choose a school that is not in the immediate locality: the time to travel in search of a school and in transporting a child over any distance, the availability of cars, childcare support and, in the last resort, the capacity to move house. Choice imposes costs that are likely to be prohibitive for many families. As emerging evidence indicates, for many families, certainly in rural areas, the promise of choice is regarded cynically as empty rhetoric. To lack resources is to be disenfranchised from the polity of the market.

Thus whatever commodities are exchanged it is the unique social functions of the market that are of fundamental importance. The market is formally neutral but substantively interested. Individuals come together in competitive exchange to acquire possession of scarce goods and services. Within the market place all are free and equal, differentiated only by their capacity to calculate their self-interest. Yet, of course, the market masks its social bias. It elides, but reproduces, the inequalities that consumers bring to the market place. Under the guise of neutrality, the institution of the market actively confirms and reinforces the pre-existing social class order of wealth and privilege. The market is a crude mechanism of social selection. It can provide a more 'effective' social engineering than anything we have previously witnessed in the post-war period.

A prisoners' dilemma?

When education thus acquires the trappings of the commodity market, with relative advantage appropriated by some at the expense of others, we may grasp the social processes that produce and reproduce this commodity. The price of positional goods and the currency of relative advantage through competition is created by and in the interests of the powerful in society. Competition entrenches the status quo and the power of the privileged few. Individuals appear to be caught in a cage.

Why is it that individuals are trapped into acting within the rules of a game they did not produce and cannot influence, when enacting the rules can only disadvantage them? A system of spiralling disadvantage and advantage ensues, which contracts the extent and scope of choice and opportunity. What is an anarchy for all but a few individuals necessarily becomes a certainty for just those few.

The paradox of a system designed to enhance choice yet producing constraint derives, so it is argued, from the internal contradictions of the education market: its institutional and social limits. The institutional limits of the market follow because it creates a 'prisoners' dilemma' for its participants (Jonathan, 1990; Miliband, 1991). Individuals are trapped into diminishing their own welfare because the mechanism prevents them from purposively coordinating their preferences to mutual advantage. Self-interest is self-defeating, and private choice irredeemably diminishes public welfare.

Hirsch's analysis of education as a positional good perhaps serves only to reinforce the social limits to market choice. Education is, he proposes, necessarily a zero-sum game: 'what winners win, losers lose'. On this analysis, expanded education produces frustration for individuals and external costs for society in its inexorable screening function. Because the function of education, according to this view, is to differentiate the population, any attempt to provide 'more education for all leaves everyone in the same place', or neglects the screening function by creating more equality:

> it is a case of everyone in the crowd standing on tiptoe and no one getting a better view. Yet at the start of the process some individuals gain a better view by standing on tiptoe and others are forced to follow if they are to keep their position. If all do follow, whether in the sightseeing crowd or among job seeking students, everyone expends more resources and ends up in the same position.
>
> (Hirsch, 1977, p. 49)

This intensified positional competition lengthens the obstacle course in search of preferential credentials and has 'the effect of . . . favouring those best able to sustain a longer or more costly race. They are the well off and the well connected' (Hirsch, 1977, p. 50). Society takes longer and spends more to sort out the 'necessary' hierarchy of achievement. The ensuing inflation of educational credentials creates, it is argued, a waste of resources that society cannot afford, and a desire for goods that cannot be met.

Expectations have been raised that cannot be fulfilled. The Malthusian Hirsch counsels society to create a different moral order, which manages social expectations more skilfully so as to take the steam out of competition and dissolve mounting frustration. According to this view a society in which all knew their place would not be a society out of sorts with itself!

Does the institutional mechanism of market competition interact with the purported nature of education – as a positional good – to create a social system beyond repair? The institutional and social characteristics of markets are, on the contrary, not fixed and unalterable but *chosen* to serve social and political purposes. The market is not a neutral mechanism but constituted to alter the relations of power in order to change society.

The polity, the market and civil society

The market is a political creation, designed for political purposes, in this case to redistribute power in order to redirect society away from social democracy and towards a neoliberal order. The market in education is not the classical market of perfect competition but an administered market. Exchange is carefully regulated, with, for example, stringent controls placed upon professional powers to redistribute resources and admissions. The market is thus an institution that is constituted by government and underwritten by legislation to define the relative powers and contractual responsibilities of participants. Thus the administered market in education seeks to fetter local elected representatives and professionals, as the bearers of the old order, and emancipate the middle class as the bearers of the new.

While some of the intended changes result directly from the introduction of market procedures to the public domain of education, other purposes emerge indirectly as a consequence of the unfolding interactions of competition. As power shifts and relationships alter the old polity becomes unrecognizable and a distinctively different political order emerges. What organizing principles characterize decision-making in the market polity and what are the consequences? Hirschman's (1970) trenchant distinction between 'exit' and 'voice' captures the very different mechanisms by which a society takes decisions about producing goods and allocating resources. Through 'exit', customers make decisions that have resource implications for supply and demand:

> The customer who, dissatisfied with the product of the firm, shifts to that of another, uses the market to defend his welfare or to improve his position; and he also sets in motion market forces which may induce recovery on the part of the firm that has declined in comparative performance. This is the sort of mechanism which economics thrives on. It is neat – one either exits or one does not; it is impersonal – any face to face confrontation between customer and firm with its imponderable and unpredictable elements is avoided and success or failure of the organization are communicated to it by a set of statistics; and it is indirect – any recovery on the part of the declining firm comes by courtesy of the Invisible Hand, as an unintended by-product of the customer's decision to shift.
>
> (Hirschman, 1970, pp. 15–16)

'Voice' expresses principles of decision-taking and allocation that are opposed in every respect to those articulated through exit:

> Voice is just the opposite of exit. It is a far more 'messy' concept because it can be graduated, all the way from faint grumbling to violent protest; it implies articulation of

one's critical opinion rather than a private, 'secret' vote in the anonymity of a supermarket; and finally, it is direct and straightforward rather than roundabout. Voice is political action *par excellence*.

(Hirschman, 1970, p. 16)

In the public sphere, however, exit becomes the mechanism for making allocative decisions. Collective 'choices' arise from the aggregation of emergent private decisions. Exit becomes, by implication, a form of political choice. The market, by determining the distribution of winners and losers in exchange, is in effect making decisions about the allocation of resources, services and power. Policy, therefore, is made through uncoordinated piecemeal decisions of private individuals. Policy is whatever people do, how they behave. If consumers dislike something their views can only be expressed implicitly but unmistakably through exit and an alternative purchase – if such is available or accessible.

The market as a result places collective welfare beyond the reach of public deliberation, choice and action: in other words, democracy. It uses exit to hold voice at bay, substituting the power of resources for the power of the better argument in public discourse. In principle, a community is denied the possibility of clarifying its needs and priorities through the processes of practical reason, in which judgements are formed about what is in the public good based on reasoned argument that leads towards practical collective choices that are monitored, revisable and accountable to the public. In particular, the disadvantaged are denied the possibility of deliberating upon and determining their life chances.

By removal of the pattern of social relationships and the emergent structures of power and wealth from the possibility of critical scrutiny civil society is separated from the polity. The market entrenches the powerful beyond control. A community that inserts exit in place of voice in the public domain and so narrows the scope of its democratic discourse to the negative freedoms of the market place is more truly, *pace* Hayek or Chubb and Moe, on the road to serfdom.

The moral order of natural selection: an ideological mask

Markets institutionalize an unequal game of winning and losing, with the winners imposing their power on the losers without redress because of the structure of social selection. Markets produce survivals and extinctions in a Darwinian zero-sum game of social class and 'natural' selection (see Sen, 1992a). Markets are politics, that is, a way of making decisions about power in society, and they ensure that the already powerful win decisively, empowering the middle class to escape whatever public voice emerges from an attenuated democratic process.

The market polity colludes in promoting the agency and choice of the public while actually extinguishing it, and while indicating radical change is actually entrenching a traditional order of authority and power. Why does the public appear to collude in its own downfall? Because the market can parade under the guise of neutrality while any ensuing inequality can hide beneath the illusion that because the agents have acted they must also have assented (cf. Jonathan, 1990).

The market polity, by reinforcing only the interests of a minority, rests on a limited and thus vulnerable legitimacy. The emphasis upon rights and an ensuing order of natural selection reveals the struggle to clothe the polity with a legitimating moral authority while removing the social order from democratic scrutiny (Hayek, 1944; Oakeshott, 1962; Anderson, 1992).

The new right, in espousing these organizing principles of competitive exchange, is therefore either naive or dishonest. Either it is ignorant of all the evidence that markets inescapably create inequality or it understands perfectly the effects of competition and has developed a rhetoric of choice to bamboozle a supposedly unwitting public. In a more open moral order there would be debate about the possibility of reconciling the purported virtues of the market – in its responsiveness, flexibility, decentralized knowledge – with the recognition of its vices in creating inequality. Moral philosophers such as Dworkin (1985) acknowledge the dilemma by arguing the case for markets but also for redistribution to place limits upon inequality: 'market allocations must be corrected in order to bring some people closer to the share of resources they would have had but for . . . various differences of initial advantage, luck and inherent capacity'.

CONCLUSION: DISCOVERING THE CHALLENGE FOR THE PUBLIC DOMAIN

Markets cannot resolve the problems we face: indeed, they ensure that we stand no chance of solving them. Those problems derive from the transformations of the time: the restructuring of work; environmental erosion; the fragmentation of society. They raise questions about what it is to be a person, what is the nature of the community, what kind of polity we need to secure the future well-being of all. These present issues of identity, well-being, rights, liberty, opportunity and justice. These predicaments cannot be resolved by individuals acting in isolation or by 'exit', because we cannot stand outside them. Markets can only exacerbate these problems: they ensure that we stand no chance of solving them and are unlikely to be legitimated by the majority of people who will be defeated and excluded by markets.

The predicaments of the time are collective or public in nature and require public action to resolve them. As Dunn (1992) argues, 'In the face of the obscure and extravagantly complicated challenges of the human future, our most urgent common need at present is to learn how to act together more effectively.' The challenge is to renew the authority of the public domain by strengthening democracy (Barber, 1984; Mouffe, 1992; Held, 1993). Only the public domain can solve the physical problems of the environment – the conditions for which lie in collective action. Only the public domain can solve the moral and social problems facing our society: issues of membership, recognition, value, space, opportunity, having a purpose for living a life. What are the qualities of the public domain that provide the conditions for resolving these issues?

- A process that enables individuals and groups to articulate and reconcile the values and needs that are believed to be central to their own development as well as that of the communities in which they live; this is inescapably a political process.
- It requires a commitment to learning, listening, reasoning and judging the public as well as private good.
- Institutions that support and sustain discourse, learning and public choice.

These institutional conditions are those of democracy and government. The structure of the public domain that best provides the conditions for motivating people to engage in individual and collective development lies in *democracy*, because democracy enables the (political) process of articulating and reconciling differences and thus establishing the conditions (individual and collective) for living a life in which all citizens can flourish, which acknowledges their values, accords them identity and sustains them materially.

Developments that became preconditions for the educational development of many young people – bilingual teaching, a multicultural curriculum, equal opportunities for a gender-neutral learning, comprehensive schools – did not emerge from Whitehall or from isolated individual assertion but bottom-up through local discourse and public action in response to articulated demands about the need to learn and an understanding of the conditions for learning. The challenge for our time is to reconstitute the conditions for a learning society (Ranson, 1986, 1992c) in which all are empowered to develop and contribute their capacities.

Note

1. The narrative of this paragraph and the following two paragraphs draws directly on material provided by Dr Bob Morris.

Chapter 6

Towards Education for Democracy:
The Learning Society

FROM THE OLD ORDER TO THE NEW

Two apparently different strategies for restructuring education and the post-war polity – corporatism and consumerism – have been developed since the mid-1970s in response to the upheavals facing late-twentieth-century society. Their effects are, however, the same, constituting a differentiated education service with opportunities regulated into a hierarchy of opportunity that limits the possibility of most developing their powers and capacities. Once more education is becoming a privilege rather than a right that underpins a shared citizenship. An élite rather than an equal democracy appears as the new principle chosen to inform and guide the polity through the transition. Such a strategy, however, seems unlikely to acquire the lasting legitimacy that characterized the social democratic project, which lasted for a generation. Yet, at the same time, there can be no returning to the original social democratic order if the predicaments of the transition are to be resolved and the presuppositions of an alternative order defined.

Even those committed to the success of the social democratic project began to acknowledge the need for reform (see Blunkett and Jackson, 1987; Marquand, 1988). Despite undoubted achievements, the 1970s crises brought into sharper focus than hitherto the limitations of the post-war era. Questions finally arose about its limited conception of education and, underlying all, the constraints imposed upon the project by the polity. The defining aspirations remained uncompleted. Equality of opportunity was still mediated by 'the stubborn resistance of class', with the children of the service class benefiting much more than those of the working class (Halsey *et al.*, 1980); disadvantage was often too narrowly defined, excluding issues of gender, race, disability and sexuality; poverty remained, and was increasing by the 1970s.

This caused some to focus attention inwards upon aspects of the process of teaching and learning that may have reduced the motivation that is the key to achievement: the overly cognitive curriculum or the meritocratic system of assessment designed to fail as much as to pass. Perhaps even the best purposes of education were rather narrowly conceived – 'a child-centred schooling'. To define an education as that of the child in 'the classroom' within the safe boundaries of 'a school' was to contradict the originating purposes of creating an educated public.

More profound limitations lay in the organizing principles and assumptions of the period. These assumptions – of professional expertise and control – were in fact the defining conditions of the welfare and social democratic state as it was conceived at the time (cf. Perkin, 1989). To begin to question the practice of these professionals at that time would be to doubt the underlying assumptions of the polity. These were that the charter – as constituted by the settlement – for a just and open society to improve the well-being of all its members could be *provided* and, as it were, 'handed down' to the public. The good society or an educated public were to be *delivered* by knowledge-able specialists rather than lived and created by the public with the support of professionals. A passive public in awe of the knowledge of the active professional would receive the conditions for a new and better world. This very idea of 'welfare provision' was thus arguably flawed in conception because it divided professional and public in what could only be a shared process of transforming public health or education. It rendered artificial and abstract something that could only have significance through the practice of participation, which would have enabled 'services' to be experienced and owned as the public's.

As it was, when the cuts came in the 1970s the public did not appreciate them as a rationing of 'their' services. The lack of resistance, arguably, reflected not only a lack of attachment to services that were formally constituted as public but also a much broader alienation from 'public space'. Litter or the vandalizing of public buildings reflect an awareness that the space is not the public's. It is not something over which they believe they have any discretion and thus any sense of responsibility, which would allow them to invest anything of themselves in the public space. It is space for which a 'specialist' will take care. The public enters the space of the public domain only on the terms of the professional and as a means to satisfy individual wants defined by the professional.

THE PREDICAMENT FACING THE NEW ORDER

The predicament we face is that although the problems confronting society are public and require a public solution, our society has developed institutions that are not con-stituted to encourage an active public domain. The characteristics of structural change in society (fragmentation, privatism and sectionalism) and the qualities of the market order (atomism, self-interest and competition) mutually reinforce the erosion of public life and thus the conditions for personal autonomy as well as collective well-being. The qualities of the social democratic past (specialization, paternalism and passivity) pro-vide no refuge either.

The vacuum in the polity is a public of active citizens. The challenge for our time is to renew the purposes and institutions of democracy, which allows citizens to participate in the creation of a society that enables each to develop as a person but also to contribute to the good of the community as a whole. Civic responsibility and individual develop-ment are perceived as mutually reinforcing, creating the conditions in which 'anyone might do best and live a flourishing life' (Aristotle). Change depends upon new institu-tional reforms that can tie educational purpose to renewal of the public domain. The task is to re-create, or create more effectively than ever before, a public and an educated public that has the capacity to participate actively as citizens in the shaping of a learning society and polity.

The predicament we face, however, is that although the problems confronting society are public and require a public solution, our society is denigrating and dismantling the very conditions necessary to sustain its future welfare. We live in a society whose institutions are not constituted for, but require, public participation and cooperation. For some (e.g. MacIntyre, 1987) what we require may be beyond our reach. The creation of an educated public presupposes qualities and relations that have been eroded ineluctably by the specialization of the modern world.

For MacIntyre, the remaking of an educated public has been the 'presupposed telos of our modern educational system', yet it cannot be realized. For him, 'teachers are the forlorn hope of the culture of Western modernity' because the mission with which they are entrusted 'is both essential and impossible'. MacIntyre argues that although our future depends upon the re-creation of an educated public, 'what modernity excludes is the possibility of the existence of an educated public'. Moreover, the purposes presupposed in modern educational systems – of introducing young people into membership of an educated public – are also inherently undermined. Preparation for and membership of an educated public presupposes the existence of a community, a public 'which is no longer available'. The specifically modern qualities of specialization have eroded not only the idea of a public but also the idea of a thinking public, so much so that what MacIntyre regards as the two main tasks of modern educational systems are now inherently incompatible: preparing young people for some role in society, and enabling them to think for themselves. The one is now inherently a preparation for specialism, whereas the other implies public activity. The two tasks can only be combined, it is argued, when the exercise of a role itself requires mastery of a culture that requires each young person to speak for himself or herself, and that capacity is only possible within an educated public. For thinking, it was clear to Kant, is a public activity in that it presupposes use of and agreement about standards of rational activity that shape the process of justification in discourse. Thinking, for Kant, is not a specialized, professional activity, but one requiring a general culture of public discourse:

> To be enlightened is to be able to think for oneself; but it is a familiar truth that one can only think for oneself if one does not think by oneself. It is only through the discipline of having one's claims tested in ongoing debate, in the light of standards on the rational justification of which the participants are able to agree, that the reasoning of any particular individual is rescued from the vagaries of passion and interest.
>
> (see MacIntyre, 1987, p. 24)

Kant could not have conceived of a context in which thinking – even about the most general public concerns, about the nature of justice and the good society – could be 'deformed' into a specialized activity and handed over to professionals. Yet that is what has happened in modern society: the educated public has been replaced by a heterogeneous set of specialized publics.

MacIntyre's pessimism may derive from the overly narrow preconditions he places upon what constitutes an educated public. To agree with the defining conditions is inevitably to be drawn into a conclusion that the future is doomed. Can an educated public be other than as MacIntyre conceives it? His exemplar is the educated public created by the universities in early-eighteenth-century Scotland. At that historical moment the distinctive identity of Scottish institutions (the law, education, the Church) required vindication in the face of anglicization as well as Gaelic, Catholic and Episcopalian influences. The creation of such an identity, and through it of an educated public, was initiated through the universities by the Principal of Edinburgh. Within the universities and then in wider public forums there arose a distinctive mode of debate, which generated what is properly termed an educated public. Three characteristics came to define the educated public. First is a large number of individuals educated into the habit and the opportunity of active rational debate, to whose verdict appeal is made from intellectual protagonists. The individuals understand that they constitute a public and that the issues debated have a practical implication for the community in which they live: 'thus an educated public is to be contrasted both with a group of specialists, participation in whose controversies is restricted to their peers, and with a passive public of readers or listeners who merely provide an audience for the debates of others' (p. 18). Second, the debates were shaped by an agreed understanding of what form the dispute would take, what constituted a rational justification, as well as shared assent to the principles it was reasonable to appeal to and against which the argument would be judged. Such principles defined the subject matter of moral philosophy. Third, the public shared background beliefs and understanding of canonical texts as well as a tradition of interpretive understanding.

The debates in society came to resemble those of the seminar room or the journal. That 'a large segment of a whole society should institutionalize its informal debates over the best way for its members to live, so that the conversation of that society is to some extent an extension of and an interchange with the discussions within its universities, also that that same truth is to that degree exemplified in society at large, is a relatively rare phenomenon'. Its conditions were not only the influence of the university curriculum, and shared assent to modes of debate, but also an understanding by members of the educated public of their social roles; that is, of their responsibilities to the wider society in local forums, councils, boards and courts to look beyond immediate questions to issues of first principles.

The conditions MacIntyre sets for citizenship in the public domain are unnecessarily pessimistic. The requirements of debate in the philosophy seminar room may be an ideal to strive for although even there essentially contested methodologies may frustrate communication. Moreover, it would be to consider the logical terms of debate to be the precondition for understanding the meaning of another's communication. This surely places unduly restrictive terms upon human discourse. The conditions of Habermas's 'communicative rationality', whereby, in unfettered contexts, people can explore the integrity of their accounts in order to reach shared understandings, are demanding ones and will require institutional settings that promote reason in public discourse. Institutions matter. They make a difference to the purposes and course of human interaction. They are not determined but can – must – be chosen. The challenge now is to create the institutional settings that support the creation of a public domain committed to very different values and purposes. After all, that is the positive message of MacIntyre's story: the historical context of a society confronting a crisis of identity in the face of competing social, cultural and political influences. The diversity had to be clarified and interpreted to enable a new authoritative order to emerge, and this depended upon the generation of new institutional arrangements.

These are the conditions of our own times. If the transformations are to be coped with a new polity is required that enables more active public participation and discourse to generate the legitimate foundation for any new moral and political order. The need can generate the institutional prerequisites for a broader and more active educated public.

TOWARDS THE LEARNING SOCIETY

The challenge for the time is to create a new moral and political order that responds to the needs of a society undergoing a historic transition. The limitations and contradictions of the post-war polity, together with the flawed conception implied in the present neoliberal restructuring, begin to suggest the presuppositions for any new order that is to gain the consent of the public as a whole.

The creation of a moral and political order that expresses and enables an active citizenship within the public domain is the challenge of the modern era. The task is to regenerate or constitute more effectively than ever before a public – an educated public – that has the capacity to participate actively as citizens in the shaping of a learning society and polity. This will require citizens, both as individuals and together, to develop a much firmer sense of their agency (which Macmurray (1953) defines as the reflective subject in action), both in the creative development of the projects that are to define the unfolding of their lives and in their active contribution to the social and political life of the community as a whole. The prerequisite of agency can begin to illuminate the foundations of a new moral and political order.

However, the very possibility of tying together a morality that sets out the principles about how we are to live with a just polity that constitutes how we are to agree a future is strongly contested. For Rorty (1989), there can be no way of creating a comprehensive theory that brings together the private world of self-creation and the public world of justice. They are incommensurable. However, Nagel (1990) and Raz (1986) argue – more persuasively I believe – the necessity of perceiving their mutual dependence, especially at the present time. Each is a condition for the other. Public good depends upon private values, which involve, as Nagel says, 'the moral hold that the lives of others in general have upon us'. For him, there can be no just democracy without a deeply ingrained moral culture that 'leads us to impose on ourselves limits to the pursuit of our interests, limits which we believe everyone ought to observe'. Raz is clear, furthermore, that the conditions for self-creation and autonomy are public and collective. The autonomy of each depends upon the restraint of all. While these conditions depend upon what Berlin (1969) called 'the negative freedom' of individuals to experience the space within which to develop their individuality, they also require (what Berlin resisted) the 'freedom to' develop their capacities. Personal development depends upon public virtue. Freedom depends upon justice. Autonomy requires the moral and political conditions that enable each person to develop his or her powers so that public goods, such as education, 'are constitutive of the very possibility of autonomy' (Raz, 1986, p. 207).

The theory that can provide the common language of agency to enrich a new moral and political order is that of citizenship within the learning society. The notion of a citizen captures our necessary duality as individuals and as members of the public. The deliberative agency of the citizen is exercised in judgement, in choice and in action so that his or her powers and capacities are actively and reflectively expressed through the creative development of the self, through civic virtue within the community and through discourse within the polity.

Key components of the theory of the learning society

These ideas for a theory of the learning society build upon thinking and emerging practice in some parts of the country. Reforms do not begin *de novo*, they have their origins in local communities that are discovering solutions to dilemmas they confront. Our task is to develop an understanding of underlying principles in order to create the basis for their more general application.

The theory builds upon three axes: of presupposition, principles and purposes. The presupposition establishes an overarching proposition about the need for and purpose of the learning society; the principles establish the primary organizing characteristics of the theory; purposes and conditions establish the agenda for change that can create the values and conditions for a learning society.

Presupposition

There is a need for the creation of a learning society as the constitutive condition of a new moral and political order. It is only when the values and processes of learning are placed at the centre of the polity that the conditions can be established for all individuals to develop their capacities, and that institutions can respond openly and imaginatively to a period of change. The transformations of the time require a renewed valuing of and commitment to learning: as the boundaries between languages and cultures begin to dissolve, as new skills and knowledge are expected within the world of work and, most significantly, as a new generation, rejecting passivity in favour of more active participation, needs to be encouraged to exercise such qualities of discourse in the public domain. A learning society, therefore, needs to celebrate the qualities of being open to new ideas, listening to as well as expressing perspectives, reflecting on and enquiring into solutions to new dilemmas, cooperating in the practice of change and critically reviewing it.

Principles

Two organizing principles provide the framework for the learning society: that its essential structure of *citizenship* should be developed through the processes of *practical reason*.

Citizenship establishes the ontology, the mode of being, in the learning society. The notion of being a citizen ideally expresses our inescapably dual identity as both individual and member of the whole, the public; our duality as autonomous persons who bear responsibilities within the public domain. Citizenship establishes the right to the conditions for self-development but also a responsibility that the emerging powers should serve the well-being of the common wealth. I define citizenship (cf. Held, 1989) as the status of membership of national and local communities which thereby bestows upon all individuals equally reciprocal rights and duties, liberties and constraints, powers and responsibilities. Citizens have the right as well as the obligation to participate in determining the purposes and form of community and thus the conditions of their own association.

Practical reason establishes the epistemology, the mode of knowing and acting, of the citizen in the learning society. Practical wisdom (or what Aristotle called 'phronesis') describes a number of qualities that enable us to understand the duality of citizenship in the learning society: knowing what is required and how to judge or act in particular situations; knowing which virtues should be called upon. Practical reason, therefore, presents a comprehensive moral capacity because it involves seeing the particular in the light of the universal, of a general understanding of what good is required as well as what proper ends might be pursued in the particular circumstances. Practical reason, thus, involves deliberation, judgement and action: *deliberation* upon experience to develop understanding of the situation, or the other person; *judgement* to determine the appropriate ends and course of action, which presupposes a community based upon sensitivity and tact; and learning through *action* to realize the good in practice.

Purposes, values and conditions

To provide such purposes and conditions, new values and conceptions of learning are valued within the public domain at the level of *the self* (a quest of self-discovery), at the level of *society* (in the learning of mutuality within a moral order) and at the level of *the polity* (in learning the qualities of a participative democracy). These conditions for learning within the self, society and the polity are discussed in turn.

Conditions for a learning self

At the centre of educational reforms within the inner city as much as those emerging from the polity itself is a belief in the power of agency: only an active self or public provides the purposes and condition for learning and development. By creatively expressing his or her qualities and powers each citizen develops what is distinctively unique about him or her as a person. Gould (1988) emphasizes the continuous process of learning implied in the cultivation of capacities:

> The process of self-development thus consists in the formation of new capacities and in the elaboration or enrichment of existing ones. In this process, individuals may be said to widen their range of actions and social interactions and intensify or improve the quality of particular modes of action or social relation. The development of intellectual, moral or artistic capacities, or of practical and technical skills, as well as the cultivation of forms of social relations such as friendship and cooperation . . . in this development of capacities, individuals may be said to achieve greater freedom of action in the wider range of choices that are opened for their action and in the power to realise their purposes which their increased competence affords. Such a cultivation of capacities is a relatively long term or continuous process.
>
> (Gould, 1988, p. 47)

This emerging self-assertion and autonomy of the agent develops not in isolated events but in the creative shaping of a life, during the course of which capacities can be transformed. Three conditions are proposed for developing purpose and capacity within the self: a sense of agency; a revived conception of discovery through a life perceived as a unity; and an acknowledgment of the self in relation to others.

The self as agent

Learning requires individuals to progress from the post-war tradition of passivity, of the self as spectator to the action on a distant stage, to a conception of the self as agent in both personal development and active participation within the public domain. Such a transformation requires a change from self-development for occupation to self-development for autonomy, choice and responsibility across all spheres of experience. The change also presupposes moving from our prevailing preoccupation with cognitive growth to a proper concern for development of the person as a whole – feeling, imagination and practical/social skills as much as the life of the mind. An empowering of the image of the self presupposes unfolding capacities over (a life) time. This implies something deeper than mere 'lifelong education or training' (referred to by access to institutions). Rather it suggests an essential belief that an individual is to develop comprehensively throughout his or her lifetime and that this should be accorded value and supported.

The unity of a life

We need to recover the Aristotelian conception of what it is to be and to develop as a person over the whole of a life and of a life as it can be led (see MacIntyre, 1981; Archbishop Temple, quoted in Butler, 1982). This has a number of constituent developments. First is perceiving the life as a whole: the self as developing over a lifetime. Second, therefore, is a conception of being as developing over time: life as a quest, with learning at the centre of the quest, to discover the identity that defines the self. Third is seeing the unity of a life as consisting in the quest for value, each person seeking to reach beyond the self to create something of value, which is valued. Fourth is developing as a person towards the excellences: perfecting a life that is inescapably a struggle, an experience of failure as well as success. Fifth is accepting that the struggle needs to be guided by virtues, which support the development of the self: dispositions that strengthen and uplift (character); valued dispositions. Sixth is acknowledging that the most important virtue is that of deliberation, a life of questioning and enquiry committed to revising both beliefs and action; learning, from being a means, becomes the end in itself, the defining purpose creatively shaping the whole of a life.

The self as a person in relation

But we can only develop as persons with and through others; the conception of the self presupposes an understanding of how we live a life with each other, of the relationship of the self to others; the conditions in which the self develops and flourishes are social and political. The self can only find its moral identity in and through others and membership of communities. Self-learning needs to be confirmed, given meaning by others, the wider community. What is of value will be contested. Therefore we need to agree with others what is to be considered valuable; to deliberate, argue, provide reasons.

The social conditions for learning

The unfolding of the self depends upon developing the necessary social conditions to provide a sense of purpose within society, for both the self and others. These conditions are *civitas*, active participation in creating the moral and social order, and a capacity for interpretive understanding.

Virtues of civitas: *the civic virtues of recognizing and valuing others, of friendship*

The conditions for the unfolding self are social and political: my space requires your recognition and your capacities demand my support (and vice versa). Jordan (1989) emphasizes the importance of mutual responsibility in developing conditions for all individuals to develop their unique qualities. This recalls Aristotle's celebration of civic friendship – of sharing a life in common – as being the only possible route for creating and sustaining life in the city. Such values, arguably, are now only to be found within feminist literature, which emphasizes an ethic of caring and responsibility in the family and community, and the dissolution of the public as a separate (male) sphere (see Gilligan, 1986; Pateman, 1987; Okin, 1991). It is only in the context of such understanding and support that mutual identities can be formed and the distinctive qualities of each person can be nurtured and asserted with confidence.

Creating a moral community

The post-war world was silent about the good, holding it to be a matter for private discretion rather than public discourse. But the unfolding of a learning society will depend upon the creation of a more strenuous moral order. The values of learning (understanding) as much as the values that provide the conditions for learning (according dignity and respecting capacity) are actually moral values that express a set of virtues required of the self but also of others in relationship with the self. The values of caring or responsibility, upon which can depend the confidence to learn, derive any influence they may have from the authority of an underlying moral and social order. The civic virtues, as MacIntyre (1981) analyses, establish standards against which individuals can evaluate their actions (as well as their longer 'quest'); yet particular virtues derive meaning and force from their location within an overall moral framework (what MacIntyre calls a 'tradition'). A moral framework is needed to order relationships because it is the standards accepted by the moral community that provide the values by which each person is enabled to develop.

However, a moral order is a public creation and needs to be lived and re-created by all members of the community. Each person depends upon the quality of the moral order for the quality of his or her personal development and the vitality of that order depends upon the vitality of the public life of the community. For the Athenian, the virtuous person and the good citizen were the same because the goods that informed a life were public virtues. But the authority of a moral order for the modern world will grow if it is an open morality rather than a socializing into a tradition. The development of a moral community has to be a creative and collaborative process of agreeing the values of learning that are to guide and sustain life in the community.

Interpretive understanding: learning to widen horizons

Taylor (1985, 1991, 1992) has argued that the forms of knowing and understanding, as much as (or at least as part of) a shared moral order, are the necessary basis of civic virtue. Historically conditioned prejudices about capacity, reinforced by institutions of discrimination, set the present context for the learning society. The possibility of mutuality in support of personal development will depend upon generating interpretive understanding; that is, upon hermeneutic skills which can create the conditions for learning in society: in relationships within the family, in the community and at work. In society we are confronted by different perspectives, alternative life-styles and views of the world. The key to the transformation of prejudice lies in what Gadamer (1975) calls 'the dialogic character of understanding': through genuine conversation the participants are led beyond their initial positions, to take account of others and move towards a richer, more comprehensive view, a 'fusion of horizons', a shared understanding of what is true or valid. Conversation lies at the heart of learning: learners are listeners as well as speakers.

The presupposition of such agreements is *openness*: we have to learn to be open to difference, to allow our pre-judgements to be challenged; in so doing we learn how to amend our assumptions and develop an enriched understanding of others. It is precisely in confronting other beliefs and presuppositions that we are led to see the inadequacies of our own and transcend them. Rationality, in this perspective, is the willingness to admit the existence of better options, to be aware that one's knowledge is always open to refutation or modification from the vantage point of a different perspective. For Gadamer, the concept of *Bildung* describes the process through which individuals and communities enter a more and more widely defined community: they learn through dialogue to take a wider, more differentiated view, and thus acquire sensitivity, subtlety and capacity for judgement.

Reason emerges through dialogue with others: through which we learn not necessarily 'facts' but rather a capacity for learning, for new ways of thinking, speaking and acting. Habermas (1984) articulates the conditions for such communicative rationality as being 'ideal speech contexts' in which the participants feel able to speak freely, truly, sincerely. The conditions for this depend upon the creation of arenas for public discourse – the final and most significant condition for the creation of the learning society.

Conditions in the polity

The conditions for a learning society are, in the last resort, essentially political, requiring the creation of a polity that provides the fundamental conditions for individuals and the communities in which they live to develop their capabilities and to flourish. This is the moral purpose of the polity as articulated by Aristotle (Nussbaum, 1990, 1992; Sen, 1992b; Nussbaum and Sen, 1993). The personal and social conditions, described above, will be hollow unless bedded in a conception of a reformed, more accountable, and thus more legitimate, political order that empowers the public. The connection between individual well-being and the vitality of the moral community is made in the public domain of the polity: the good (learning) person is a good citizen. Without political structures that bring together communities of discourse, the conditions for learning will not exist: it is not possible to create the virtues of learning without the forms of life and institutions which sustain them. The preconditions of the good polity are justice, participative democracy and public action.

Justice: a contract for the basic structure

The conditions for agency of self and society depend upon agreement about its value as well as about allocating the means for private and public self-determination. Freedom rests upon justice, as Rawls (1971, 1993), Barry (1989), Nagel (1991) and Sen (1992b) argue. But this makes the most rigorous demands upon the polity, which has to determine the very conditions on which life can be lived at all: membership, the distribution of rights and duties, the allocation of scarce resources, the ends to be pursued. The good polity must strive to establish the conditions for virtue in all its citizens: material (for example, clean public water); institutional (for example, education); and moral (a civic ethic). There issues are intrinsically political and will be intensely contested, especially in a period of transformation that disturbs traditions and conventions.

If decisions about such fundamental issues are to acquire the consent of the public then the procedures for arriving at those decisions will be considered of the greatest significance for legitimate authority of the polity. The process of making the decisions – who is to be involved and how the disagreements that will inexorably arise are to be resolved – will be as important as the content of decisions themselves.

Participative democracy

Basing the new order upon the presupposition of agency leads to the principle of the equal rights of citizens both to participate in determining what conditions the expansion of their powers and to share responsibility for the common good. The ancient Athenians believe that every citizen could take part in the democratic process because the art of political judgement (without which there could be no civilized society) was something that all ordinary people were capable of. Politics could not be for specialists alone.

The political task of our time is to develop the polity as a vehicle for the active involvement of its citizens, enabling them to make their contribution to the development of the learning society. There is a need, in this age of transition, to fashion a stronger, more active democracy than the post-war period has allowed (Pateman, 1970; Macpherson, 1973, 1977; Lively, 1975; Barber, 1984, 1988; Keane, 1984, 1988a, b; Green, 1985; Held, 1987, 1991, 1993; Arblaster, 1987; Gould, 1988; Simey, 1988; Mouffe, 1992; Dunn, 1992; Phillips, 1991, 1993). The post-war polity specialized politics and held the public at bay except periodically and passively.

The principle that constituted classical democracy, of 'proper discussions' – of free and unrestricted discourse, with all guaranteed a right to contribute – needs to be restored in a form appropriate to the modern world. The aim would be to enable all to contribute to public discourse, the purpose of which is to ground decisions in the force of the better argument. The challenge is to restore a culture that values the practice of public discussion and the open giving and taking of reasons as grounds for conclusions (see Dunn, 1992).

The constitutive condition for citizenship within a more active democracy is a polity that enables the public to participate and express their voice about the issues of the transition, but also a polity that will permit public choice and government (Ranson and Stewart, 1989, 1994). The politics of public expression but also the government of choice and action is the challenge for the new polity. Within such a polity the procedures for involving the public and for negotiating decisions will be important, yet it is through the prerequisites of procedural justice (see Habermas, 1984; Haydon, 1987; Gould, 1988; Hampshire, 1989) that an educated public of citizens can emerge. Citizens need to acquire the dispositions of listening and taking into account as well as asserting their view.

> The deliberative process of democratic decision-making requires that each participant not only permit the others to express their views and offer their judgements but take others' views seriously into account in arriving at his or her own judgement. Clearly this does not require agreement with the views of others, but rather serious attention to, and respect for, their views. Such reciprocal respect also presupposes that disagreements be tolerated and not suppressed.
>
> (Gould, 1988)

By providing forums for participation the new polity can create the conditions for public discourse and for mutual accountability so that citizens can take each other's needs and claims into account and learn to create the conditions for each other's development. Learning as discourse must underpin the learning society as the defining condition of the public domain.

Public action

For the Athenians democracy formed a way of life. Citizens were deeply involved in public affairs and took part in the government of their community, while acknowledging the separateness of each person as important ethically. Citizens grasp the necessary duality of autonomy and interdependence, realizing that excellence can only be worked out with and through others in a moral community. The contemporary world, by contrast, has emphasized the autonomy of each individual at the expense of their shared membership, interdependence and responsibility for the public domain.

A more active citizenship, Mill believed, would be a civilizing force in society. Through participation citizens would be educated in intellect, in virtue and in practical activity. The upshot of participation should now be public action based upon deeper consent than that obtained from earlier generations. For Sen (1990; Dreze and Sen, 1989) the possibility of producing a fairer world, one that will enrich the capacities and entitlements of all citizens, depends upon the vitality of public, democratic action. The creation of a learning society expresses a belief in the virtue of the public domain and will depend upon the vitality of public action for its realization.

The value of ordinary people serving the needs of others in the community in which they live and work may often take the form of voluntary activity. Titmuss (1971) and

Simey (1988) recognize that the importance of voluntary service in the community lies in the expression and encouragement of responsible citizenship, of citizens taking ownership of and responsibility for the life of the community. The principle of voluntarism strengthens the polity as well as the common welfare of all. The ultimate conditions for mutuality, however, lie in public action within the forums of the polity to establish justice for all.

REFORMING GOVERNMENT FOR THE LEARNING SOCIETY

The structure of government will need to be reformed if it is to enable the learning society. What framework of government is, therefore, appropriate to the needs of the learning society? I will consider the organizing principles for a more democratic framework and then set out the functions and powers of the tiers of government within a new structure of partnership.

Organizing principles for democratic governance

The government of education should be constituted according to the following principles of organization.

For the public good

Education is a public service constituted to enable an educated and educating public domain – open, just and democratic, respecting and involving the capacities of all citizens. The organization of education can facilitate or frustrate the creation of an open, learning society. Private education denies the possibility of such a polity: it divides the educating of young people, so that those in the 'independent' sector acquire a hidden curriculum of power, a closed world behind the boundaries of protected exclusiveness. Respect and mutual cooperation cannot be developed in a polity where young people are segregated in their educating along the class divide (see Tawney, 1931). Guidelines for the government of the learning society need to begin by celebrating education as a public good and challenging the enclaves of private power to take down the boundaries.

Enabling participation for civic purpose

The challenge for education as it approaches the twenty-first century is to enable the public as citizens to contribute to the development of their own society. If equality and quality are to be assured then decisions about institutional arrangements, resourcing, staffing and curriculum development need to flow from a process of democratic and cooperative planning between the partners. Public choice needs planning if the results are to reflect the needs of all. The task is to discover a solution that eschews either professional corporatism or market self-interest, and this challenge of realizing public choice that is sensitive to diversity can only find its solution in processes that are much more democratic as well as collaborative than we have accomplished hitherto. The creation of community forums, councils and advisory panels can enable public discourse and tie participation into the processes of representative democracy.

Progressive decentralization

The relations between central and local government should be guided by the principle of progressive decentralization in order to allow greater participation at every level in the government of the learning society. Yet if the principles of a new polity and society are to be accomplished authority will need to be organized appropriately at every level, according to the principle of subsidiarity with decisions always taken at the lowest tier commensurate with efficiency. We need to be clear about the tasks to be undertaken as well as to understand the limits of government at different tiers: in short we need a theory of power and authority that analyses the distribution of powers to different tiers to fit their appropriate responsibilities and tasks.

- At the centre, power is needed to determine the infrastructure of national public policy in education: its purposes, its learning principles, its frameworks, its resourcing and its role in inspection and quality assurance.
- At the level of local governance, power is needed for the strategic planning and development of the systems of learning, institutional frameworks, networks of participation, public dialogue and quality assurance.
- At the level of institutions within the community, power is needed to enable local partnerships to form in support of individual and community participation to discuss and negotiate an education that empowers them as citizens. The powers of each of the other tiers of government have their rationale in enabling the vitality of learning and participation at this level.

Thus responsibilities and powers should be distributed to each interdependent tier of education – the centre, the local authority, institutions and the community – so that each can make its appropriate contribution to the shared overall purposes of the learning society by enabling autonomy and citizenship through a system of comprehensive and equal opportunities. The direction of power distribution is towards decentralization but also towards partnership and mutual answerability.

Multiple accountability

The principles of polycentrism and partnership from the period of social democracy need to be restored and further developed in any reformed government of education. The bureaucratic centralization constituted by the ERA needs to give way to the understanding once more that public services need to acknowledge plural centres of power – centre, locality, institution and community – which must collaborate if the needs of all are to be met. The new partnerships require greater commitment than in the past to cooperative working and also to multiple accountability: willingness both to give an account of purposes and to be held to account on the exercise of responsibilities.

What implications do these several organizing principles have for a new structure to the government of education, at the levels of central government, of local government, of the school and the college, and of the parent and the community?

Structure: central government

A new Department of Education and Training should be created to integrate the functions of personal and skill development now differentiated between two Whitehall Departments – the Department of Employment and the Department for Education. Even from a labour market perspective individuals require a much broader conception of continuing development at an advanced level if they are to provide for the needs of the emerging high-tech service economy. At present, each department without the proper influence of the other will inevitably encourage too narrow a conception of the capacities needed for personal development, will duplicate innovation and deny integrated accountability.

The distinctive function of central government is to develop the purposes, principles and structures that provide the necessary conditions for the development of the learning society. The task for the centre is to prepare the national framework, the infrastructure for quality and equality in education, rather than to prescribe the detail of institutional form or the content of the learning process. These are the proper responsibilities of the LEA and the teachers working in partnership with parents and the community. The primary *functions* of the centre, therefore, are to:

- enable and promote national policy for the learning society;
- develop the infrastructure;
- develop strategic planning and resourcing;
- commission research;
- evaluate the quality of learning.

Enabling and promoting

The classical view of the DFE has emphasized its role in the *promotion* of national policy. More recently, Glennerster (1983) has supported the effective impact of the Department upon the climate of opinion in education 'through a rather intangible but very real shift in the balance of prevailing values'. What is now to be promoted? A principal task for the new DET should be to use this proven capacity to shape opinion and values by promoting the very notion of public education.

The Department will have an essential role in coordinating the development of national policy. But because the education service must inescapably work through partnership the task of the centre is often to *enable* the partners to contribute to and share in the creation of national policy. Two organizational developments need consideration to supplement this role of the DET. First, there is a need to recreate the Advisory Councils (Robbins, Newsom, Plowden, etc.), which were a progressive influence in post-war education policy. The function of these councils is, at key moments, to draw together the disparate policy community in education to create a common language and shared understanding of the key policy issues. Whitehall would complain that this process is too slow, but the agreed proposals would prove longer lasting than instant policy-making in the heat of the political moment.

Second, there will be a need to create an integrated National Curriculum and Assessment Council, representative of the partners and radically revised in responsibilities. Curricula need to be adapted to meet the needs of the learner and thus to be open to the informed judgement of the local partners about the desired ideas and practices that should influence the curriculum. The proper role of the DET is to establish principles which form a framework for learning:

1. Values of educational purpose
    *   equality of educational opportunity;
    *   personal growth and confidence;
    *   a multi-cultural and anti-prejudice society;
    *   community education and development;
    *   citizenship and democracy.
2. The aims of learning
    *   to help children develop lively enquiring minds;
    *   to instil respect for moral values, for other people and oneself;
    *   to help children understand the world;
    *   to help children use language effectively;
    *   to provide a basis of mathematical, scientific and technological knowledge.
3. Curriculum design
    *   areas of learning experience (human and social, linguistic and literary, mathematical, moral, physical, scientific, spiritual, technological);
    *   elements of learning (knowledge, concepts, skills, attitudes), 'an empowerment curriculum';
    *   characteristics of learning (learner-centred, active learning, breadth, balance, relevance, progression and continuity), 'investigative learning'.
4. Formative as well as summative assessment.
5. Pastoral care and counselling key to the curriculum: 'a negotiated curriculum'.

The centre, therefore, has an important task: to enable the partners to reach agreement about the characteristics and qualities of learning and then to generate understanding of good practice. The role of the centre is then to promote ideas, innovations and practices that have been developed by teachers and LEAs to reform the quality of learning in schools, colleges and the community. The challenge for the Department is to help to stimulate and circulate the creative reforms that invariably grow up from the roots of the service.

Developing the infrastructure

The role of promotion will in this way complement and reinforce the department's major function, to constitute the infrastructure nationally for public comprehensive education. Three policies will be required to dissolve the market and regenerate the conditions for educational equality:

*   end the grant-maintained/CTC sector;
*   phase out the private sector;
*   end the voluntary sector.

The most difficult task for the new DET will be to forge a settlement between the state and the private and voluntary sectors. Richard Pring (1987) has described the various ways in which private schooling is subsidized by public funds. There are obvious forms of state subsidy through the assisted places scheme, but there are also more disguised forms of subsidy through the charitable status of independent schools, which exempts them from paying taxes (on profit from fees) or national insurance (exemption from employer's surcharge) and gains them rate relief. Even more indirect support comes from the charitable status of non-educational institutions that can support private schools, or the corporate sector purchasing fees and places at such schools for its employees. A new settlement would begin by offering financial incentives to the private sector to join the public sector, progressively reducing the subsidizing of independent schooling.

Butler's compromise between Church and state in 1944 was a major achievement. But there is growing understanding of the need for the state to review the settlement with the voluntary sector because of the problems caused by falling school rolls as well as the growth of a multi-faith, multicultural society. In the past the *Times Educational Supplement* has argued that there was a need to prepare the ground for new legislation. The argument for change derives from the need to establish democratic control over a sector that can operate hidden selective admission policies while the need to create a multicultural society would seem to require either that all the faiths can opt for denominational schooling or that all should give up their independence in the interests of a more integrated, though plural, society. The latter option now presents the stronger claims.

Developing strategic planning and resourcing

While the accelerating centralization of power in Whitehall needs to end and be significantly reversed, it is nevertheless appropriate for the DET to be accorded the necessary 'steering capacity' to implement agreed national policy.

There is a need to restore the process of strategic development planning between central and local government. All LEAs would be required to submit to the DET a plan for the development of education in their areas. The plan would include a statement of strategic policy objectives for: the aims of the service; reforming teaching and learning; a design for curriculum and assessment; the pattern of institutional organization; and how they intend to involve parents and community. Post-16 continuing education and training would be expected to form a large part of the development plan.

The plans would conform to a cycle of the kind the DES recommended for school development planning (DES, 1989), which is now widely regarded as good practice:

- auditing of quality and quantity (reviewing strengths and weaknesses);
- constructing the plan (clarifying strategic priorities, plans and targets);
- implementation of the planned priorities to agreed targets;
- evaluation: the quality of achievement is checked.

These plans would be negotiated with the Department, which should require that they complied with the principles and guidelines expressed in national policy. The DET would not be involved in determining the detail of plans. While it could require an LEA to have a policy plan that followed guidelines on equal opportunities, it could not define the detailed programme. By controlling the process, the DET would seek to encourage good practice.

Where exemplary practice emerged, the DET could work with these LEAs in order to develop understanding of the policies and practices for national dissemination. The DET would continue to use educational specific grants to promote and steer good practice locally.

Commissioning research

Research is vital to the quality of progress within the education service. Policy developments in the service should always be underpinned by the knowledge and understanding provided by major research. (The Research Branch of the ILEA was a national institution informing the educational community as a whole.) The DET needs to establish an education research council that can sponsor major programmes of research into issues of equality, teaching and learning, community education, professional development, etc.

Evaluating the quality of education

Monitoring and evaluating the quality of learning and institutional performance must be central to the education service at all levels. The process of external evaluation requires local authorities and their institutions to submit their practice to the critical examination of inspectors. The process of inspection ensures that practice is compared to the best experience elsewhere and is made public and accountable to the wider community.

HM Inspectorate provided an invaluable service and needs to be restored. Its judgement is widely respected and its quasi-independence has been used to make challenging comments about the quality of education nationally as well as locally. The publicizing of reports has strengthened its public influence: a critical account can prompt the partners to swift remedial action. HMI, however, is a professional body. There is a need for its work to be complemented and extended by a Quality Council. Such a Council, representative of the partners, would enable a national and public debate about achievement and performance in education. Its debates would draw upon research as well as HMI reports.

The extraordinary extension of powers sanctioned by the 1988 Education Reform Act needs to be reversed. Unlimited power in Whitehall counters the move towards a more participatory democracy. The centre needs those powers which are appropriate to its functions of establishing the purposes and infrastructures of the nation's public education service – but not powers to intervene in detail.

Thus retaining section 1 of the 1944 Education Act, without powers of detailed intervention, restores the relationship between central and local government that obtained prior to the mid-1970s. That is, the Department was required to work in partnership with local government because although it had overall responsibility it could not determine the detail. Civil servants complained that this was intolerable because it provided them with authority bereft of power and it made for slow implementation of change. Nevertheless, partnership is better than authoritarian centralism, and time for consultation is the beneficial price of accountable democracy.

Structure: local government

The central questions facing the reform of educational government surround the LEA: should local government have a role in education and, if so, what should be its proper functions? In the period of social democracy the LEA became arguably the key arm of planning post-war reforms, in particular the movement for creating a comprehensive system of schools that would enable all young people to experience educational, and thus career, opportunities previously reserved for a privileged minority. LEAs saw their role as providing the buildings, staff and resources that would establish the infrastructure of opportunities for teachers to practise their professional skills within schools and colleges to develop the powers and capacities of young people. The LEA, known as the 'maintaining' or 'providing' LEA, had wide-ranging responsibilities for providing a comprehensive service in its area, not only for the three stages of learning – primary, secondary and further – but also for the community as a whole ('to contribute towards the spiritual, moral, mental and physical development of the community, by securing that efficient education throughout those stages shall be available to meet the needs of the population of their area': s. 7, 1944 Education Act). Although the LEA had responsibility for the curriculum (s. 27, 1944 Act), issues of learning process were typically regarded as professional matters for heads and their teaching staffs in schools and colleges. LEAs developed and administered the framework of education while delegating the content and quality of learning to others.

The achievement of the 1988 Education Reform Act was to propose that this traditional focus was now misplaced and that the energies of the LEA, if it was to have any role in the future scheme of things, ought to concentrate upon ensuring the quality of learning in schools and colleges – by monitoring and evaluating the implementation of the National Curriculum. Learning quality and accountability to parents and the public were now the primary functions of the LEA, rather than direct provision and administration of services. A continuing strategic role of leading the system was open to the LEA if it could achieve the confidence of schools, colleges and the community. It is clear from case studies (Ranson, 1992a) that LEAs have responded positively both to the challenge of redirection and to achieving a leadership based upon the management of influence. Whereas the traditional role of the LEA was to provide and maintain the administrative and institutional infrastructures for schools and colleges, now the overriding mission of the local education authority is to reform the process of learning, enhance the quality of achievement and promote a new relationship of service and accountability to the public. These values are complemented by a new understanding of management as strategic leadership of a service founded upon partnership.

Recent work (Ranson, 1992a; Cordingley and Kogan, 1993; Simon and Chitty, 1993) suggests that local government has a quite indispensable role to play in developing equality of opportunity and quality of learning in a democratic society. While future reforms can build upon the positive developments contained within the 1988 Education Reform Act, some of the functions and constitutive powers need to be restored to the local government of education to enable it to fulfil a more powerful brief than accorded to it in recent legislation. The case for the local government of education rests upon three arguments.

1. Learning is inescapably a *system*: learning is a process that cannot be contained within the boundaries of any one institution. Discovery and understanding occur at home, in the community, on a scheme of work experience as well as in college or school. Progress, furthermore, will unfold more securely between stages of learning when they are mutually comprehending and supporting. Improved achievement, it is proposed, depends for its realization upon enabling a wider system of learning: one element cannot be treated in isolation from another if each is to contribute to the effective working of the whole. For every school, the appropriate numbers of pupils, the provision of resources and teachers to support a balanced and comprehensive curriculum, with choices at key stages to enable progression in response to diversity of need, are requirements that have to be managed at the level of the system as a whole, as well as the school, if all young people are to be provided with opportunities to realize their powers and capacities.

2. Education needs to be a *local* system: the system of learning is more effective if managed locally, as well as nationally and at the level of the institution. The different tasks need their appropriate tier of management and by creating a local system that delegated *and* enabled strategic leadership, the 1988 reforms enacted the conditions for excellence in the local management of education within a national framework. A local system of management is needed to ensure understanding of local needs, responsiveness to changing circumstances and efficiency in the management of resources within geographic boundaries consistent with identifiable historical traditions. Such local systems need to be properly accountable and this requires location within a local democratic system.

3. Education needs to be a local *democratic* system: if education is, as it should be, a public service of and for the whole community rather than merely the particular parents, young people and employers who have an immediate and proper interest in the quality of the education provided, then education must be responsive and accountable to the community as a whole. The significance of learning for the public as a whole suggests the indispensable location of the service within a framework of democratic local government that enables all local people to express their views and to participate actively in developing the purposes and processes of their education service. A learning society – enabling all to contribute and respond to the significant changes of the period – will depend for its vitality upon the support of local democratic institutions that articulate and take responsibility for developing all members of community.

A flourishing public domain requires the vitality that local democratic governance brings to education. Upon local authorities lies the inescapable task of both reinterpreting national purpose to local need and generating the shared sense of purpose that is the precondition for public confidence and commitment. Only a very sophisticated social institution could bring off this demanding task. The challenge for the future is to extend, rather than extinguish, the qualities of equality and justice within local democracy.

New reforms need first to celebrate the principle of local democracy and government of education. The LEA is not a tier of administration, or a separate tier: it is an integral part of a major institution of democracy in our society. Education will benefit from stronger rather than weaker local government. To this end a multi-purpose local authority of the kind proposed by the Redcliffe-Maud Commission (1969) is needed to restore the *structure* of local governance linking town and country, incorporating health and water, and having an all-round responsibility for the safety, health and well-being, both material and cultural, of people in its locality. The focus of this strengthened local government would be upon the strategic planning and development of the public services within its area, including school and college building, hospitals, housing, environmental health and other services. The functions of the strategic authority would be to establish the infrastructure, the foundations for more participation within the community. At this level representative democracy draws together the diversity of local perspectives and ensures collective decisions for action that are clear, legitimated and accountable.

The local education authority is central to the vision of this new strategic local government. Its task is to prepare a development plan that both articulates the purposes of the national framework and expresses the ambitions for citizenship in the learning society as expressed within local communities and their institutions. This vision of the local government of education must constitute an integrated set of institutions serving local democratic education. Just as any national framework would make little sense if a local authority could opt out, so the local government of education fails to make any consistent sense if institutions are allowed to opt out at will. Members of the public domain cannot stand outside their responsibilities for the public domain. The challenge for the future is for all to make attractive and rewarding the public space in which all must live and flourish. If problems exist, as no doubt they will, at a local level, in relationships between an authority, its institutions and the public, then they have to be addressed in other ways, as they are when they are experienced at a national level, in the appropriate procedures and tribunals of public accountability.

This structure of a unified and integrated public education service led by a strong and strategic LEA at the centre will need to be complemented by a framework of community councils and institutional governing bodies that are accorded the delegated decision-making powers that are appropriate to the functions and responsibilities of democratic community governance.

This structure constitutes a much more complex network of participation in decision-making than hitherto. Although the reformed local government of education will restore its institutional unity and coherence, the tradition of hierarchical control will remain a thing of the past. The local authority will relate to a more diffuse system of councils, institutions and agencies and, although it will be accorded greater 'steering capacity' than under the 1988 Education Reform Act, it must, nevertheless, largely seek to influence and to work in partnership with rather than to direct. But this is to begin to describe the functions of the new LEA.

The primary *function* of the local government of education is to enable the unfolding of the learning society within an LEA's area of responsibility. Its task is to provide strategic leadership that will encourage the local education partners to develop a shared understanding of learning quality, of the system of management and of public service and accountability.

A vision of learning

The functions of the LEA in developing the system of learning can be summarized once more as follows. Working within the national framework, it must develop a vision of equality and quality in educational opportunity for all in society throughout their lives: it is now understood more clearly that unless the service carries equality of opportunity into the heart of the learning process then many young people will experience barriers to the full development of their capacities. Perhaps a charter of pupil rights can set out their entitlement to expect diversity of cultural heritage to be celebrated and valued, a learning environment free from prejudice and discrimination, and a commitment of classroom and school to social justice. It must also reform the organization and process of learning so as to give all students access to a broad and balanced curriculum through strategies that encourage active and flexible approaches to learning and teaching to enable progression within and between the stages of education.

The LEA therefore has a leading role to play in generating understanding of and the conditions for processes of learning that will release the powers and capacities of adults as well as young people and encourage them to make their responsible contribution to the development of their society.

Strategic planning and resourcing

The LEA has the key function of ensuring that there is cohesion and direction in the promotion of the local vision of education through the articulation of interdependent development plans from every part of the service, which express specific objectives while taking account of the local authority's mission. In this way LEA policy statements about, for example, supporting the special learning needs of the disadvantaged can be given expression and resource advantage throughout the service as a whole. It will be a key role of the local government of education to approve the development plans of the constituent parts of the service.

Resource distribution throughout the education authority will reflect the policy objectives expressed in the strategic plan, with specific grants targeting chosen priorities for innovation and development. Formulae for funding institutions and centres will be calculated on the basis of need rather than the per capita (quasi-voucher) system implemented in the Education Reform Act.

Employment and provision

To ensure consistency and efficiency in staffing policy, the LEA should: be involved in senior staff appointments; be the staffing agency for teachers; and have a right to place one in ten teachers in order to carry out redeployment and avoid waste of teacher skills. The LEA should play the lead role in planning the in-service development of staff throughout the service. The scale of the strategic LEA can ensure cost-effective provision of services to support the school curriculum, specialist services to children with special needs, as well as the provision of youth, adult and community services that are indispensable both to the quality of mainstream schooling and, of course, to the broader ambitions of the learning society.

Support

Increasingly the task of the new LEA is not to provide services but to offer support and advice to the providers, enabling them to realize the priorities set out in their development plans. This may require the LEA to give specialist financial, legal and personnel advice as well as to play the role of consultant to improve the process of devolved management. The focus of advice changes. In the past advisers provided advice and support to teachers in their subject departments rather than to heads and the management of schools. Increasingly the 'scope of advice and support will be enlarged, the diagnosis of educational problems must go deeper and the destination of advice and support will be more directed at heads, principals and particularly governing bodies' (interview with a Kent local education authority officer).

Evaluating quality

Parents, employers and the wider community are entitled to excellence as well as access in public services and it is one of the principal functions of the LEA to monitor and evaluate all the services within its responsibilities to ensure the highest quality of performance. The LEA must have a strategic role in: assuring the quality of learning, identifying and disseminating good practice in curriculum development and teaching method; encouraging clear and consistent thinking throughout the service about educational values and purposes; making staff development suit the needs of institutions by encouraging good management; and, especially, developing a system of monitoring and evaluation that encourages schools and colleges to review their performance and complements this with processes of evaluation that assure the public of the quality of teaching and learning. Many LEAs are developing new perspectives and systems to assure the quality of their service: perhaps a 'whole school audit approach' to monitoring and evaluation, or a 'total quality programme' that pervades the whole organization. A key role for the LEA is to identify and develop good practice and achievement in the learning process, to act as the catalyst and promoter of excellence by sponsoring research and innovation.

Partnership and networking

The challenge for the new LEA is to develop a strategic leadership based upon a process of working in partnership with a multiplicity of organizations. It requires the LEA to develop a culture of shared responsibility and collaborative working that encourages institutions to trust in more permeable boundaries. New forms of organizational arrangement are being developed which seek to devolve administrative decision-making to schools but also to local areas: either to formally constituted local area offices or to informal networks of institutions working in partnership to develop the curriculum and the resources that make it possible. The new LEA will be more decentralized than before so that it can become more responsive to the needs of schools and colleges but also to the articulated needs of parents, employers and the community. At the same time the leadership role of the LEA will be to draw together and interpret the diversity of 'voices' from the service and its public so as to clarify strategic priorities and choices for the future direction of the service.

Enabling participation, voice and accountability

The most important partnership the new LEA has to enable is that with parents, employers and the wider public, to ensure that services are provided which meet their needs, to report on the quality of those services and, most significantly, to engage the public in a discussion about the purposes and process of education in the learning democracy. The procedures of accountability need to enable the diversity of 'accounts' to be expressed and mediated. The role of the LEA is to set up, enable and support the more devolved institutional arrangements of democratic participation in education.

Together these functions of the local government of education identify an increasingly complex challenge of facilitating a much more enriched conception of the learning society than has been the case traditionally: one that facilitates the responsible participation of citizens, a culture of deliberation and action for the common good as well as personal development.

    Although the LEA should not return to a mode of detailed and hierarchical administrative control of the local education service, it should be a unified although differentiated service, and should be accorded appropriate powers to steer the system as a whole in just the same way that Whitehall should be accorded steering capacity to ensure some unity as well as diversity in the national education service. Powers appropriate to the strategic responsibilities of the LEA should include:

- to determine the local institutional system (in partnership with the centre);
- to approve the development plans of institutions and centres;
- to determine the formulae for resource distribution;
- to determine specific grants;
- to identify, with the local partners, policy priorities of positive discrimination;
- to determine senior staff appointments;
- to determine the in-service training budget.

The LEAs' deployment of such powers will grow in authority and legitimacy the more the policies they seek to implement are derived in association with the local partners, so that there is a shared understanding of the purposes and plans for development of the service as a whole.

Structure: institutions, schools and colleges

Any programme of reforms to the local government of education needs to build upon the achievements of the 1988 Education Reform Act in strengthening the authority and quality of schools and colleges. But the emphasis in that legislation of encouraging schools and colleges to see themselves as isolated, inward-looking islands of learning needs to be dissolved in favour of values that support the contribution the institution can make to learning in the life of the community as a whole. Schools would continue to be led by strong governing bodies, whose membership represents all the local partners, including parents, students and the local community, and whose functions would be to govern, within the guidelines of LEA priorities, the preparation of a development plan that supports the distinctive needs of the school or college while contributing to local institutional networks.

The central challenge at the level of the institution is to enable reform of the learning process. In communities experiencing entrenched disadvantage and underachievement a conception of the appropriate purposes and conditions of learning has been developing over time. The problem has been defined as the deep sense of hopelessness and loss of self-esteem, dignity and confidence: 'something has to be done to remove the stigma and feeling of cynicism and helplessness so evident on the estates'. The problem is essentially one of 'how people on low incomes are treated and made to see themselves and their capabilities – living down to other people's expectations'. In some communities this is experienced as prejudice and discrimination as 'their' attributes (race, gender or special needs) are stereotyped and categorized.

In this context the particular challenge has been perceived as 'The long-term process of transforming the way people think about themselves and what they are capable of and of shaping our methods of implementation accordingly.' The management task has been one of clarifying a vision of learning that will enable local people to develop confidence in their powers and capacities as the basis for their own future development as well as that of the communities in which they live. In some institutions development plans have been formulated that articulate such a vision to regenerate a learning community and facilitate the management of change. The organizing principles of such an agenda in these schools and colleges are now discussed in turn (Ranson, 1992c).

Valuing capacity

Values were carefully chosen to celebrate a distinctive vision about the reservoirs of capacity in individuals: the purpose of education being to create active rather than passive learners, empowered with the skills to make responsible choices about the direction of their own lives as well as to cooperate with others to improve the quality of life for all in the community. The educators believed in:

1. *Valuing all individuals equally*, ensuring that education gives 'equal value and care to all children, young people and adults regardless of sex, ethnic origin, disability, social and economic status or level of attainment'.
2. *Valuing the identity and dignity of each*, to develop the self-esteem that is a precondition for learning. Education helps young people to form positive attitudes to themselves as well as others and thus to dissolve prejudice.
3. *Belief in individual capacity and achievement*: 'that no limit should be assumed to the individual's capacity for achievement: this must be the basis of expectations of all children and young people from all backgrounds.' Believing in the capacities and achievements of young people across all areas of experience is perceived as a precondition for learning.
4. *Valuing agency, assertiveness, self-confidence*: to learn is to reach out, to examine something beyond the self; to encounter a different environment and the strangers within it. The value of self-confidence is especially important for those groups – girls, the black and ethnic minorities – which have, traditionally, been disadvantaged by education. One headteacher of an all-girl school reinforced these arguments: 'The value of self-confidence cannot be stressed enough: the ability to communicate with others, both known and strangers, in different environments, to be able to go out into the world, mix with others, be able to project and stand up

for themselves. . . . We want girls to be proud of being female and be aware that they can enter any profession they wish and that they can play a major role both in the school and in the world outside. This school wishes to ensure that girls will leave equipped with the skills to speak up for themselves, to be assertive and to question. You have this history of girls being passive and seen as well behaved and "very good students" because they sit in a corner and read and copy out. But actually when they are tested they can do poorly. I think passivity is a great danger. Girls unfortunately have a history of being told to shut up while the male speaks, whatever culture they come from. We have to build up the self-esteem and self-confidence of girls.' Black students are similarly being encouraged to learn to question and to challenge: for example, the way their history is being taught, whose history is being presented, what is missing and why it has been excluded.

5. *Agency: empowerment for autonomy and responsibility* enables children to become independent learners. They manage what they are doing, make decisions about the best way of doing it and have access to resources: 'Students need to be able to think and act for themselves so that they can achieve the maximum control over their lives; helping students to become self-reliant, self-motivating and autonomous so that they can make decisions for themselves.'

6. *Responsibility for others and the wider community*. The educators wished to encourage an outward looking education: 'Schools and colleges should help young people to form constructive and cooperative attitudes to each other, to their work and to the community so that they can play an active and responsible role in society.' There was also some movement towards active citizenship and an understanding of the importance of taking decisions.

Provision for entitlement

A number of values established objectives for schools and colleges: what is offered in terms of opportunities, resources and facilities. Thus it was argued that provision should enable the principles of: *entitlement* to a comprehensive and continuing education for all to achieve personal growth throughout their lives; *responsiveness* to the expressed educational needs of all in the community; *accessibility* to enable members of the community to take up learning opportunities, which require *flexibility* of provision in schools and especially in further and higher education to enable students to transfer between courses and maintain *progression* in learning. *Resources* remain a vital condition for educational quality and these LEAs invested considerably in staff development; indeed, they strove to protect expenditure in the face of pressure to contract it. A belief in *quality development* was expressed in the growing commitment to the monitoring and evaluation of provision.

Teachers and advisers sought to develop principles that would encourage a comprehensive curriculum that would be *relevant* to learners, enabling them to draw upon their experience of living within the community. This proposed curriculum should be broad and balanced in the learning offered, *modular* in its form, though ensuring *coherence* and integration across the experience of learning, enabling *continuity* and *progression*, and supporting young people with *formative and positive assessment* to help them understand their achievements and progress.

Active learning

If learning is to be effective it should motivate young people by engaging their interests and by being relating to their experience. The process of teaching, moreover, should seek to involve students in, and negotiate with them, a process of active and collaborative learning: 'we must shift from a teaching approach to a learning approach'. The values emphasized:

1. *Student-centred learning*: education should begin from the needs and strengths of the individual and not merely the benchmarks of preconceived standards; 'learning should be appropriate to the needs of individual pupils and provide a challenge to each one'. 'We must take time and involve students, to share the ownership of learning. It is no good if the "problem" is ours and we tell the answers. It is only when the child owns a problem in learning that they will really want to learn "to write" or "to read". We need to listen to children.'
2. *Participation and dialogue*: motivation is more likely if learning grows out of a process of agreeing with pupils the tasks to be undertaken.
3. *Active learning*: there is a strong belief among educators in disadvantaged LEAs that if the learning process is to be involving it needs to be a more active experience than it has proved traditionally in most schools. Active learning can encourage students to take responsibility for their own learning experience and that of others.
4. *Learning can serve others*: learning, even within the traditional subject curriculum, can be given purpose by serving the needs of others in the community.
5. *Collaborative learning*: if students are to achieve the educational value of respecting other persons and cultures, then the very process of learning must encourage collaborative as well as individual activity. Pupils need to be given responsibility of developing projects together so that they decide the ends and plan the means: 'Learning is most fulfilling as a cooperative activity rather than a solitary or competitive enterprise.' Your ideas and knowledge provide the spark to my discovery, your progress is necessary to mine.
6. *Learning as enjoyment*: 'Learning should be interesting and challenging, it should be an exciting experience. It should be fun. Too many schools are still boring environments.'

Partnership with parents and the community

Partnership with parents is regarded as the key to improving pupil motivation and achievement, while service to and the involvement of the public reflects the broader responsibility of school and college to promote education within the community. Characteristics of partnership for improving learning quality include:

1. *Welcoming parents into the life of the school as partners*: establishing a new style in which schools will listen to and respond to parents – 'as teachers we need to listen, learn and respect. The great mystique about teacher autonomy needs to be unmasked.'
2. *Parents as complementary educators.* In the home: parental contribution to schemes of reading is encouraged because of its acknowledged influence upon

motivation, confidence and attainment scores. In school: they increasingly recognize the wide range of skills and experience among parents, which can support the learning process.

3. *Developing shared understanding of the curriculum*: establishing a closer match of understanding within the partnership takes time, given the differences of perception, but 'teachers, pupils and parents as well as others need to know what is intended, how it is to be pursued and achieved'.

4. *Dialogue in curriculum design*: listening to parents and members of the community about how the curriculum, enriched by local knowledge and experience can enhance a school's multicultural and anti-racist understanding.

5. *Partners in assessment of learning progress*: establishing regular communication with parents about the progress their child is making; involving the parent in assessment and in agreeing a strategy about future development.

6. *Partners in evaluation and accountability*: schools having the confidence to report to parents about performance, to listen to the 'accounts' of parents and to involve them in evaluating achievement.

Structure: parents and the community

The purpose of all the reforms is to enable a learning society, one in which parents are as much committed to their own continuing development as they are to supporting their children's unfolding education, in which women assert their right to learn as well as support the family, in which learning cooperatives are formed at work and in community centres, and in which all are sufficiently preoccupied with the issues of the purpose and organization of learning to get involved in the public dialogue about reform.

Such a participative democracy in and for education presupposes a strong 'periphery' to education, as it does a strong LEA or state. Indeed, in the new order of things, the periphery should be perceived as the centre, with all the other tiers of government seen as circles of enabling support radiating out from the defining purpose of it all: ordinary people individually and together devoting their energies to developing their own powers and capacities but also those of the local community. Taking responsibility for the quality of the common wealth is an intrinsic value as well as being a condition for the autonomy of each.

Schools and colleges are part of such a strong area and community perspective, committed to working together so that they are more effective in listening to and responding to the articulated needs of the community. Organization is a vehicle for purpose and if the principle of participation and local responsiveness is to be firmly established then organizational mechanisms need to be developed to support the identification of local needs, facilitate participation and support the coordination of schools, colleges and centres. These mechanisms could take three forms:

1. *Community forums.* Some schools have in the past introduced such forums to extend community participation, and in some authorities forums have been established for specific purposes: for example, to review proposals for school reorganization, or more generally to consider educational issues. A stronger democracy

suggests the need for community forums with a wider remit, to enable parents, employers and community groups to express local needs and share in decision-making about provision to meet them.

2. *Grant-giving capacity.* Public dialogue about educational reform is properly a primary responsibility of community forums, but they should be able to exert influence and a limited resource-giving capacity (delegated by the local authority) could be deployed in support of the learning needs of individuals and groups within the community. This would be an important strategy in enfranchising and empowering community education and reinforcing the providers' responsiveness to local needs.

3. *The enabling role of the area officer.* The mutual cooperation of schools, colleges and centres in support of the learning society will sometimes happen spontaneously. It is likely to be accelerated by the support area officer or adviser, who encourages parental and group involvement in identifying learning needs and in deciding upon and organizing appropriate development projects. Monitoring and evaluating progress and enabling the dialogue of accountability are crucial activities in the role. It is a networking role, in which the officer, or local community representative, works to link up the parts of the service so that the authority and its institutions can make an integrated response to the needs of parents and the community. The role becomes the *animateur* of the community as an educational campus.

CONCLUSION

A beleaguered service is variously accused of failing young people who leave school at the earliest opportunity with much of their potential unrecognized and underdeveloped. A more practical curriculum tied to the world of work is proposed by some as the solution most likely to provide the required motivation to learning for those pupils. But this proposal turns an effect (the school curriculum) into the focus of policy, thus obscuring the real (social and political) causes. Moreover, the proposal is confused: for unless the vocational reform is for all children then it becomes another policy that will reinforce the social selection it is purportedly designed to overcome.

Education will always 'fail' if the capacity of young people has to be sectioned off to match a pyramidal, hierarchical society (the hidden curriculum of which is learned very early by young people), underpinned by a political system that encourages passive rather than active participation in the public domain. A different polity, enabling all people to make a purpose of their lives, will create the conditions for motivation in the classroom. Only a new moral and political order can provide the foundation for sustaining the personal development of all. It will encourage individuals to value their active role as citizens and thus their shared responsibility for the common wealth. Active learning in the classroom needs, therefore, to be informed by and to lead towards active citizenship within a participative democracy. Teachers and educational managers, with their deep understanding of the processes of learning, can, I believe, play a leading role in *enabling* such a vision to unfold not only among young people but also across the public domain.

References

Adam Smith Institute (1984) *Omega File*. London: Adam Smith Institute.

Anderson, P. (1992) The intransigent Right at the end of the century. *London Review of Books*, 24 September.

Apple, M. (1979) *Ideology and the Curriculum*. London: Routledge & Kegan Paul.

Apple, M. (1982) *Cultural and Economic Production in Education*. London: Routledge & Kegan Paul.

Arblaster, A. (1987) *Democracy*. Milton Keynes: Open University Press.

Archer, M. (1979) *Social Origins of Educational Systems*. London: Sage.

Archer, M. (1981) Educational politics: a model for their analysis. In P. Broadfoot *et al.* (eds), *Politics and Educational Change*. London: Croom Helm.

Ball, S.J. (1990a) *Politics and Policy Making in Education: Explorations in Policy Sociology*. London: Routledge & Kegan Paul.

Ball, S.J. (1990b) Markets, inequality and urban schooling. *Urban Review*, **22** (2), 85–100.

Ball, S.J. (1992a) Schooling, enterprise and the market. American Education Research Association symposium paper, San Francisco, April.

Ball, S.J. (1992b) The worst of three worlds: policy power relations and teachers' work. Keynote address to BEMAS Research Conference, University of Nottingham, April.

Barber, B. (1984) *Strong Democracy: Participatory Politics for a New Age*. Berkeley: University of California Press.

Barber, B. (1988) *The Conquest of Politics: Liberal Philosophy in Democratic Times*. Princeton, NJ: Princeton University Press.

Barry, B. (1989) *Theories of Justice*. Volume 1: *A Treatise on Social Justice*. Hemel Hempstead: Harvester Wheatsheaf.

Bauman, Z. (1988) *Freedom*. Milton Keynes: Open University Press.

Beer, S. (1965) *Modern British Politics*. London: Faber.

Bell, D. (1974) *The Coming of Post-industrial Society*. London: Heinemann.

Bell, D. (1979) *The Cultural Contradictions of Capitalism*. London: Heinemann.

Bellamy, R. (1987) *Modern Italian Social Theory*. Oxford: Polity Press.

Benn, C. (1980) A new 11-plus for the old divided system. *Forum*, **22** (2), 36–41.

Berlin, I. (1969) *Four Essays on Liberty*. Oxford: Oxford University Press.

Bernstein, B. (1975) *Class, Codes and Control*. Volume 3: *Towards a Theory of Educational Transmissions*. London: Routledge & Kegan Paul.

Blau, P. (1964) *Exchange and Power*. New York: Wiley.

Blau, P. and Schoenherr, R. (1971) *The Structure of Organizations*. New York: Basic Books.

Blunkett, D. and Jackson, K. (1987) *Democracy in Crisis: The Town Halls Respond*. London: Hogarth Press.

Board of Education (1943) *Education Bill: Explanatory Memorandum by the President of the Board of Education*. Cmd 6492. London: HMSO.

Bogdanor, V. (1979) Power and participation. *Oxford Review of Education*, 5 (2), 157–68.

Boudon, R. (1974) *Education, Opportunity and Social Inequality*. Chichester: Wiley.

Bourdieu, P. (1977) *Outline of a Theory of Practice*. Cambridge: Cambridge University Press.

Bourdieu, P. and Passeron, J.C. (1977) *Reproduction: in Education, Society and Culture*. London: Sage.

Bowe, R. and Ball, S. with Gold, A. (1992) *Reforming Education and Changing Schools*. London: Routledge & Kegan Paul.

Briault, E. (1976) A distributed system of educational administration: an international viewpoint. *International Review of Education*, 22 (4), 429–39.

Briault, E. and Smith, F. (1980) *Falling Rolls in Secondary Schools*. Slough: NFER.

Brown, P. (1990) The 'Third Wave': education and the ideology of parentocracy. *British Journal of Sociology of Education*, 11 (1), 65–85.

Bullock, A. (1960) *The Life and Times of Ernest Bevin*, Volume 2. London: Hodder & Stoughton.

Butler, D. and Kavanagh, D. (1984) *The British General Election of 1983*. London: Macmillan.

Butler, R.A. (ed.) (1977) *The Conservatives: A History from Their Origins to 1965*.

Butler, R.A. (1982) *The Art of Memory*. Sevenoaks: Hodder & Stoughton.

CCCS (1978) Social democracy, education and the crisis. Occasional Paper No. 52, Birmingham.

CCCS (1981) *Unpopular Education: Schooling and Social Democracy in England since 1944*. London: Hutchinson.

Cheshire, T.E. (1976) Priorities in education. *National Westminster Bank Quarterly*, November.

Chubb, J. and Moe, T. (1990) *Politics, Markets and America's Schools*. Washington, DC: Brookings Institution.

Chubb, J. and Moe, T. (1992) Classroom revolution. *Sunday Times Magazine*, 9 February.

Coates, R.D. (1972) *Teachers' Unions and Interest Group Politics*. Cambridge: Cambridge University Press.

Cordingley, P. and Kogan, M. (1993) *In Support of Education: The Functioning of Local Government*. London: Jessica Kingsley.

Crewe, I. (1986) On the death and resurrection of class voting: some comment, on 'How Britain votes'. *Political Studies*, 34, 620–38.

Cruikshank, M. (1963) *Church and State in English Education*. London: Macmillan.

Dahrendorf, R. (1988) *The Modern Social Conflict: An Essay in the Politics of Liberty*. London: Weidenfeld & Nicolson.

Dale, R. (1989) *The State and Education Policy*. Milton Keynes: Open University Press.

Dale, R., Esland, G., Fergussan, R. and Macdonald, M. (eds) (1981) *Education and the State*. Volume 1: *Schooling and the National Interest*. London: Falmer Press.

Daniels, W.W. (1980) *House of Lords Select Committee 1979–80*, Volume II. London: HMSO.

DE (1943) *Educational Reconstruction* (White Paper). Cmd 6458. London: HMSO.

DE (1958) *Secondary Education for All: A New Drive*. Cmnd 604. London: HMSO.

DE (1959) *15 to 18* (The Crowther Report). London: HMSO.

DE (1963a) *Half Our Future* (The Newsom Report). London: HMSO.

DE (1963b) *Higher Education* (The Robbins Report). London: HMSO.

Dent, H.C. (1944) *Education in Transition*. London: Kegan Paul, Trench, Trubner.

DES (1965) The Organisation of Secondary Education, Circular 10, 12 July. London: DES.

DES (1967) *Children and Their Primary Schools* (The Plowden Report). London: HMSO.

DES (1970) The Organisation of Secondary Education, Circular 10/70, 30 June. London: DES.

DES (1976) *The Yellow Book*. Unpublished, but in DES Library; extracts published in *Times Educational Supplement*.

DES (1977a) *Education in Schools* (Green Paper). London: HMSO.

DES (1977b) *A New Partnership for Our Schools* (The Taylor Report). London: HMSO.

DES (1977c) *Report No. 87*. London: HMSO.

DES (1978) (The Oakes Committee on Higher Education). London: HMSO.

DES (1979a) *Proposals for a Certificate of Extended Education* (The Keohane Report). London: HMSO.

DES (1979b) *A Basis for Choice* (The Mansell Report). London: Further Education Unit. London.

DES (1979c) *Providing Educational Opportunities for 16–18 Year Olds*. London: DES.

DES (1980a) *Examinations 16–18* (Green Paper). London: HMSO.

DES (1980b) *Education for 16–19 Year Olds* (The Macfarlane Report). London: DES.

DES (1982) *17-plus: A New Qualification*. London: HMSO.

DES (1984) *Parental Influence at School*. London: HMSO.

DEs (1985) *Better Schools* (White Paper). London: HMSO.

DES (1987a) Press release, 20 November. London: DES.

DES (1987b) *Financial Delegation to Schools* (Green Paper). London: HMSO.

DES (1987c) *Grant Maintained Schools* (Green Paper). London: HMSO.

DES (1989) *Planning for School Development*. London: HMSO.

DES (1991) *Education and Training for the Twenty-first Century*. London: HMSO.

DFE (1992) *Choice and Diversity: A Framework for Schools*. Cm 2021. London. HMSO.

Doe, B. (1984) Forty years on. *Times Educational Supplement*, 20 January.

Dreze, J. and Sen, A. (1989) *Hunger and Public Action*. Oxford: Clarendon.

Dunleavy, P. (1980) *Urban Political Analysis*. London: Macmillan.

Dunleavy, P. and Rhodes, R. A. W. (1983) Beyond Whitehall. In H. Drucker (ed.), *Developments in British Politics*. London: Macmillan.

Dunn, J. (ed.) (1992) *Democracy. The Unfinished Journey: 508 BC to AD 1993*. Oxford: Oxford University Press.

Dworkin, R. (1985) *A Matter of Principle*. Oxford: Clarendon.

Echols, F., McPherson, A. and Willms, D. (1990) Parental choice in Scotland. *Journal of Education Policy*, **5** (3),

Edwards, T. and Whitty, G. (1992) Parental choice and educational reform in Britain and the United States. *British Journal of Educational Studies*, 40 (2), 101–17.

Ellis, A. and Kumar, K. (eds) (1983) *Dilemmas of Liberal Democracies*. London: Tavistock.

Elster, J. (1992) *Local Justice: How Institutions Allocate Scarce Goods and Necessary Burdens*. Cambridge: Cambridge University Press.

Fiske, D. (1978) Presidential address to the Society of Education Officers, January.

Foster, C.D., Jackman, R. and Perlman, M. (1980) *Local Government Finance in a Unitary State*. London: Allen & Unwin.

Fowler, G., Morris, V. and Ozga, J. (eds) (1973) *Decision-Making in British Education*. London: Heinemann.

Freire, P. (1972) *Pedagogy of the Oppressed*. Harmondsworth: Penguin.

Freire, P. (1974) *Education: The Practice of Freedom*. London: Writers' and Readers' Publishing Cooperative.

Gadamer, H.G. (1975) *Truth and Method*. London: Sheed & Ward.

Gambetta, D. (ed.) (1988) *Trust: Making and Breaking Cooperative Relations*. Oxford: Blackwell.

Gellner, E. (1969) *Saints of the Atlas*. London: Weidenfeld & Nicolson.

Gellner, E. (1979) *Spectacles and Predicaments*. Cambridge: Cambridge University Press.

Gellner, E. (1981) *Muslim Society*. Cambridge: Cambridge University Press.

Gellner, E. (1983) *Nations and Nationalism*. Oxford: Blackwell.

Giddens, A. (1981) *A Contemporary Critique of Historical Materialism*. London: Macmillan.

Giddens, A. (1990) *The Consequences of Modernity*. Cambridge: Polity Press.

Gilligan, C. (1986) Remapping the moral domain. In T. Heller, M. Sosna and D. Wellbury (eds), *Reconstructing Individualism: Autonomy, Individuality and the Self in Western Thought*. Stanford, CA: Stanford University Press.

Glennerster, H. (1983) *Planning for Priority Groups*. Oxford: Martin Robinson.

Goffman, E. (1974) *Frame Analysis*. Harmondsworth: Penguin.

Goldthorpe, J. (1978) The current inflation: towards a sociological account. In F. Hirsch and J. Goldthorpe (eds), *The Political Economy of Inflation*. Oxford: Martin Robertson.

Gorz, A. (1982) *Farewell to the Working Class: An Essay on Post-industrial Socialism*. London: Pluto Press.

Gough, I. (1979) *The Political Economy of the Welfare State*. London: Macmillan.

Gould, C. (1988) *Rethinking Democracy: Freedom and Social Cooperation in Politics, Economy and Society*. Cambridge: Cambridge University Press.

Grace, G. (1978) *Teachers, Ideology and Control: A Study in Urban Education*. London: Routledge & Kegan Paul.

Green, P. (1985) *Retrieving Democracy: In Search of Civic Equality*. London: Methuen.

Griffith, J.A.G. (1966) *Central Departments and Local Authorities*. London: Allen & Unwin.

Habermas, J. (1972) *Knowledge and Human Interests*. London: Heinemann.

Habermas, J. (1976) *Legitimation Crisis*. London: Heinemann.

Habermas, J. (1984) *The Theory of Communicative Action*. Volume 1: *Reason and the Rationalization of Society*. London: Heinemann.

Haddow Report (1926) *The Education of the Adolescent*. London: Board of Education.

Hall, S. (1981) Schooling, state and society. In R. Dale *et al.* (eds), *Education and the State*. Volume 1: *Schooling and National Interest*. London: Falmer.

Hall, S. and Jacques, M. (eds) (1989) *New Times: The Changing Face of Politics in the 1990s*. London: Lawrence & Wishart.

Halsey, A.H. (1978) *Change in British Society*. Oxford: Oxford University Press.

Halsey, A.H. (1986) *Change in British Society* (3rd edition). Oxford: Oxford University Press.

Halsey, A.H., Heath, A. and Ridge, J. (1980) *Origins and Destinations: Family, Class and Education in Modern Britain*. Oxford: Clarendon.

Hampshire, S. (1989) *Innocence and Experience*. London: Allen & Unwin.

Harvey, D. (1989) *The Condition of Postmodernity*. Oxford: Blackwell.

Haydon, G. (1987) Towards a framework of commonly accepted values. In G. Haydon (ed.), *Education of a Pluralist Society*. University of London Institute of Education.

Hayek, F.A. (1944) *The Road to Serfdom*. London: Routledge & Kegan Paul.

Hayek, F.A. (1973) *Law, Legislation and Liberty*. Volume 1: *Rules and Order*. London: Routledge & Kegan Paul.

Hayek, F.A, (1976) *Law, Legislation and Liberty*. Volume 2: *The Mirage of Social Justice*. London: Routledge & Kegan Paul.

Hayek, F.A. (1979) *Law, Legislation and Liberty*. Volume 3: *The Political Order of Free People*. London: Routledge & Kegan Paul.

Heald, D. (1983) *Public Expenditure*. London: Martin Robertson.

Heath, A. (1987) Trendless fluctuation: relative class voting 1964–83. *Political Studies*.

Held, D. (1987) *Models of Democracy*. Cambridge: Polity Press.

Held, D. (1989) *Political Theory and the Modern State*. Cambridge: Polity Press.

Held, D. (ed.) (1991) *Political Theory Today*. Cambridge: Polity Press.

Held, D. (1993) *Prospects for Democracy*. Cambridge: Polity Press.

Heller, A. and Fehrer, F. (1988) *The Post-modern Political Condition*. Cambridge: Polity Press.

Hewton, E. (1986) *Education in Recession: Crisis in County Hall and Classroom*. London: Allen & Unwin.

Hillgate Group (1986) *Whose Schools? A Radical Manifesto*. London: Hillgate Group.

Hinings, C.H., Leach, S., Ranson, S. and Skelcher, C. (1983) Implementing policy planning decisions. *Long Range Planning*, **18** (2), 38–45.

Hirsch, F. (1977) *The Social Limits to Growth*. London: Routledge & Kegan Paul.

Hirschman, A.O. (1970) *Exit, Voice and Loyalty: Responses to Decline in Firms, Organizations and States*. Cambridge, MA: Harvard University Press.

HMI (1986) *Report of Her Majesty's Inspectorate on the Effects on the Education Service in England and Wales of Local Authority Expenditure Policies*. London: DES.

HMI (1990) *Standards in Education 1988–89: The Annual Report of HM Senior Chief Inspector of Schools*. London: DES.

Hobsbawm, E. (1981) The forward march of Labour halted? and Observations on the debate. In M. Jacques and F. Mulhern (eds), *The Forward March of Labour Halted*. London: New Left Books.

Hood, C. (1986) *Administrative Analysis*. Brighton: Wheatsheaf Books.

Hood, C. and Wright, M. (eds) (1981) *Big Government in Hard Times*. Oxford: Martin Robertson.

Hudson, R. and Williams, A.M. (1989) *Divided Britain*. London: Belhaven Press.

Illich, I. (1973) *Deschooling Society*. Harmondsworth: Penguin.

James, P. (1980) *The Reorganisation of Secondary Education*. Slough: NFER.

Jonathan, R. (1990) State education service or prisoners' dilemma: The 'hidden hand' as a source of education policy. *Educational Philosophy and Theory*, **22** (1), 16–24.

Johnson, R. (1970) Educational policy and social control in early Victorian England. *Past and Present*, **49**.

Jones, K (1989) *Right Turn: The Conservative Revolution in Education*. London: Hutchinson Radius.

Jordan, B. (1989) *The Common Good: Citizenship, Morality and Self-interest*. Oxford: Blackwell.

Keane, J. (1984) *Public Life and Late Capitalism: Toward a Socialist Theory of Democracy*. Cambridge: Cambridge University Press.

Keane, J. (1988a) *Democracy and Civil Society*. London: Verso.

Keane, J. (1988b) *Civil Society and the State*. London: Verso.

Kogan, M. (1971) *The Government of Education*. London: Macmillan.

Kogan, M. (1975) *Educational Policy Making*. London: Allen & Unwin.

Kogan, M. (1978) *The Politics of Educational Change*. London: Fontana.

Krizner, I.M. (1973) *Competition and Entrepreneurship*. Chicago, University of Chicago Press.

Lash, S. and Urry, J. (1987) *The End of Organised Capitalism*. Cambridge: Polity Press.

Laver, M. (1986) *Social Choice and Public Policy*. Oxford: Blackwell.

Lawton, D. (1980) *The Politics of the School Curriculum*. London: Routledge & Kegan Paul.

Leach, S., Hinings, B., Ranson, S. and Skelcher, C. (1983) Uses and abuses of policy planning systems. *Local Government Studies*, **9**, 23–37.

Levacic, R. (1991) Markets and government: an overview. In G. Thompson *et al.* (eds), *Markets, Hierarchies and Networks: The Coordination of Social Life*. London: Sage.

Lindblom, C. (1977) *Politics and Markets*. New York: Basic Books.

Lively, J. (1975) *Democracy*. Oxford: Blackwell.

Locke, M. (1974) *Power and Politics in the School System*. London: Routledge & Kegan Paul.

Lukes, S. (1984) The future of British socialism. In B. Pimlott (ed.), *Fabian Essays in Socialist Thought*. London: Heinemann.

MacIntyre, A. (1981) *After Virtue: A Study in Moral Theory*. London: Duckworth.

MacIntyre, A. (1987) The idea of an educated public. In G. Haydon (ed.), *Education and Values*. Institute of Education, University of London.

McLeod, J. (1988) City technology colleges. *Local Government Studies*, **14** (1), 75–82.

Maclure, S. (1965) *Educational Documents: England and Wales 1816 to the Present Day*. London: Methuen.

Maclure, S. (1985) Forty years on. *British Journal of Education*, **33** (2), 117–34.

Macmurray, J. (1953) *The Self as Agent*. London: Faber & Faber.

Macpherson, C.B. (1973) *Democratic Theory: Essays in Retrieval*. Oxford: Clarendon.

Macpherson, C.B. (1977) *The Life and Times of Liberal Democracy*. Oxford: Oxford University Press.

Marquand, D. (1988) *The Unprincipled Society: New Demands and Old Politics*. London: Jonathan Cape.

Marshall, A. (1936) *Principles of Economics*. London: Macmillan.

Marshall, G., Rose, D., Newby, H. and Vogler, C. (1988) *Social Class in Modern Britain*. London: Unwin Hyman.

Marshall, T.H. (1964) *Class, Citizenship and Social Development*. Chicago: University of Chicago Press.

Martlew, C. (1983) The state and local government finance. *Public Administration*, **61**, 127–47.

Massey, D. and Meegan, R. (1982) *The Anatomy of Job Loss*. London: University of London Press.

Mawson, J. (1983) Explanations for the decline of the West Midlands. Working paper. CURS/INLOGOV, March, pp. 1–19.

Middlemas, K. (1979) *Politics in Industrial Society*. London: Deutsch.

Miliband, D. (1991) *Markets, Politics and Education: Beyond the Education Reform Act*. London: Institute for Public Policy Research.

Ministry of Education (1945) *A Guide to the Educational System of England and Wales*. Ministry of Education Pamphlet No. 2. London: HMSO.

Mishra, R. (1984) *The Welfare State in Crisis: Social Thought and Social Change*. London: Wheatsheaf.

Mouffe, C. (1992) *Dimensions of Radical Democracy: Pluralism, Citizenship, Community*. London: Verso.

Murphy, R. (1988) Great education reform bill proposals for testing – a critique. *Local Government Studies*, **14** (1), 39–45.

Murray, R. (1989) Fordism and post-Fordism. In S. Hall and M. Jacques (eds), *New Times: The Changing Face of Politics in the 1990s*. London: Lawrence & Wishart.

Nagel, T. (1990) Freedom within bounds. *Times Literary Supplement*, 16–22 February.

Nagel, T. (1991) *Equality and Partiality*. Oxford: Oxford University Press.

Norwood Report (1943) *Curriculum and Examinations in Secondary Schools*. London: Secondary Schools Examination Council.

Nozick, R. (1974) *Anarchy, State and Utopia*. Oxford: Blackwell.

Nussbaum, M. (1990) Aristotelian social democracy. In G. Mara and H. Richardson (eds), *Liberalism and the Good*. New York: Routledge.

Nussbaum, M. (1992) Virtue revived. *Times Literary Supplement*, 3 July.

Nussbaum, M. and Sen, A. (eds) (1993) *The Quality of Life*. Oxford: Clarendon Press.

Oakeshott, M. (1962) *Rationalism in Politics and Other Essays*. London: Methuen.

O'Connor, J. (1973) *The Fiscal Crisis of the State*. New York: St Martin's Press.

OECD (1975) *Educational Development Strategy in England and Wales*. Paris: OECD.

Offe, C. (1975) The theory of the capitalist state and the problem of policy formation. In L. Lindberg *et al.* (eds), *Stress and Contradiction in Modern Capitalism: Public Policy and the Theory of the State*. Toronto and London: Lexington Books.

Offe, C. (1984) *Contradictions of the Welfare State*. London: Hutchinson.

Offe, C. (1985) *Disorganised Capitalism*. Cambridge: Polity Press.

Okin, S.M. (1991) Gender, the public and the private. In D. Held (ed.), *Political Theory Today*. Cambridge: Polity Press.

Ouseley, H. (1988) Reforming education – equal opportunities lost. *Local Government Studies*, **14** (1), 93–103.

Oxenham, J. (ed.) (1984) *Education versus Qualifications*. London: Unwin.

Pahl, R. (1977) Collective consumption and the state in capitalist and state socialist societies. In R. Scase (ed.), *Industrial Society: Class Cleavage and Control*. London: Allen & Unwin.

Parfit, D. (1984) *Reasons and Persons*. Oxford: Clarendon.

Passmore, J.A. (1970) *The Perfectibility of Man*. London: Duckworth.

Pateman, C. (1970) *Participation and Democratic Theory*. Cambridge: Cambridge University Press.

Pateman, C. (1987) Feminist critiques of the public/private dichotomy. In A. Phillips (ed.), *Feminism and Equality*. Oxford: Blackwell.

Perkin, H. (1989) *The Rise of Professional Society: England since 1880*. London: Routledge.

Peston, M. (1982) Sir Geoffrey's framework for decline. *Times Educational Supplement*, 12 March.

Peters, R.S. (ed.) (1973) *The Philosophy of Education*. Oxford: Oxford University Press.

Phillips, A. (1991) *Engendering Democracy*. Cambridge: Polity Press.

Phillips, A. (1993) *Democracy and Difference*. Cambridge: Polity Press.

Popper, K. (1945) *The Open Society and Its Enemies*. London: Routledge & Kegan Paul.

Pring, R. (1987) Privatization in education. *Journal of Education Policy*, **2** (4), 289–99.

Pyle, D. (1976) Resource allocation in education. *Social and Economic Administration*, **10** (2), 106–22.

Ranson, S. (1980) Changing relations between centre and locality. *Local Government Studies*, **6** (6), 3–23.

Ranson, S. (1982) Central–local policy planning systems in education, Report to ESRC.

Ranson, S. (1984) Towards a tertiary tripartism: new codes of social control and the 17+. In
P. Broadfoot (ed.), *Selection, Certification and Control: Social Issues in Educational Assessment*. London: Falmer.

Ranson, S. (1985a) Contradictions in the government of educational change. *Political Studies*, **33** (1), 56–72.

Ranson, S. (1985b) Education. In S. Ranson, G. Jones and K. Walsh (eds), *Between Centre and Locality: The Politics of Public Policy*. London: Allen & Unwin.

Ranson, S. (1986) Government for a learning society. In S. Ranson and J. Tomlinson (eds), *The Changing Government of Education*. London: Allen & Unwin.

Ranson, S. (1987) Education for citizenship. *Journal of Education Policy*, **2** (3), 205–22.

Ranson, S. (1988) From 1944 to 1988: education, citizenship and democracy. In S. Ranson, R. Morris and P. Ribbins (eds), 'The Education Reform Bill', special issue of *Local Government*, **14** (1), 1–19.

Ranson, S. (1990a) *The Politics of Reorganising Schools*. London: Unwin Hyman.

Ranson, S. (1990b) Towards education for citizenship. *Educational Review*, **42** (2), 151–66.

Ranson, S. (1991) Government for the learning society. Unpublished paper for the Institute for Public Policy Research, London.

Ranson, S. (1992a) *The Role of Local Government in Education: For Quality Assurance and Accountability*. Harlow: Longman.

Ranson, S. (1992b) Education 1991. In F. Terry (ed.), *Public Domain 1991*. London: Public Finance Foundation.

Ranson, S. (1992c) Towards the learning society. *Educational Management and Administration*, **20** (1), 68–79.

Ranson, S. (1992d) Democracy and education endangered. *Times Educational Supplement*, 15 May.

Ranson, S. (1993a) Public education and local democracy. In H. Tomlinson (ed.), *Education and Training 14–19: Continuity and Diversity in the Curriculum*. Harlow: Longman.

Ranson, S. (1993b) Local democracy for the learning society. London: National Commission on Education.

Ranson, S. (1993c) Markets or democracy for education. *British Journal of Educational Studies*.

Ranson, S. (1993d) Renewing education. Paper presented to Institute for Public Policy Research/ Goldsmiths' College Research Conference or Alternative Education Policies, 25–26 March.

Ranson, S., Hinings, B., Leach, S. and Skelcher, C. (1986) Nationalising the government of education. In M. Goldsmith (ed.), *New Research in Central–Local Relations*. Aldershot: Gower.

Ranson, S. and Stewart, J. (1989) Citizenship and government: the challenge for management in the public domain. *Political Studies*, **37** (1), 5–24.

Ranson, S. and Stewart, J. (1994) *Management for the Public Domain: Enabling the Learning Society*. London: Macmillan.

Ranson, S. and Tomlinson, J. (eds) (1986) *The Changing Government of Education*. London: Allen & Unwin.

Rawls, J. (1971) *A Theory of Justice*. Oxford: Clarendon.

Rawls, J. (1993) *Political Liberalism*. New York: Columbia University Press.

Raz, J. (1986) *The Morality of Freedom*. Oxford: Oxford University Press.

Redcliffe-Maud, Lord (Chairman) (1969) *Report of the Royal Commission on Local Government in England*, Volume 1. Cmnd 4040. London: HMSO.

Regan, D. (1977) *Local Government and Education*. London: Allen & Unwin.

Rhodes, R. (1981) *Control and Power in Central–Local Government Relations*. Westmead: Gower.

Rhodes, R. (1988) *Beyond Westminster and Whitehall: The Sub-central Governments of Britain*. London: Unwin Hyman.

Robson, W. A. (1976) *Welfare State and Welfare Society*. London: Allen & Unwin.

Robson, W. W. (1950) *British Government since 1918*. London: Allen & Unwin.

Rogers, M. (1991) *Three Years of Opting Out: An Analysis*. London: Local Schools Information.

Rorty, R. (1989) *Contingency, Irony, and Solidarity*. Cambridge.

Rothwell, R. (1982) The role of technology in industrial change: implications for regional policy. *Regional Studies*, 3316 (5), 361–9.

Ryan, A. (1974) An essentially contested concept. *Times Higher Educational Supplement*, 1 February, 13.

Sallis, J. (1988) *Schools, Parents and Governors: A New Approach to Accountability*. London: Routledge & Kegan Paul.

Salter, B. and Tapper, T. (1981) *Education, Politics and the State*. London: Grant Macintyre.

Saran, R. (1973) *Policy Making in Secondary Education*. Oxford: Clarendon.

Saunders, P. (1981) *Social Theory and the Urban Question*. London: Hutchinson.

Saunders, P. (1982) Why study central–local relations? *Local Government Studies*, **8** (2), 55–62.

Sen, A. (1985) The moral standing of the market. *Social Philosophy and Policy*, **2** (2), 1–19.

Sen, A. (1990) Individual freedom as social commitment. *New York Review of Books*, 14 June.

Sen, A. (1992a) On the Darwinian view of progress. *London Review of Books*, 5 November.

Sen, A. (1992b) *Inequality Reexamined*. Oxford: Clarendon Press.

Sen, A. (1993). Capability and well-being. In M. Nussbaum and A. Sen (eds), *The Quality of Life*. Oxford: Clarendon Press.

Sexton, S. (1987) *Our Schools – A Radical Policy*. London: Institute of Economic Affairs.

SHA (1979) *Big Is Beautiful*. London: Secondary Heads Association.

Shipman, M. (1984) *Education as a Public Service*. London: Harper & Row.

Simey, M. (1988) *Democracy Rediscovered: A Study in Police Accountability*. London: Pluto Press.

Simon, B. (1964) *The Two Nations and the Education Structure 1780–1870*. London: Lawrence & Wishart.

Simon, B. (1978) *Intelligence, Psychology and Education: A Marxist Critique*. London: Lawrence & Wishart. First published 1953.

Simon, B. and Chitty, C. (1993) *SOS: Save Our Schools*. London: Lawrence & Wishart.

Skelcher, C., Leach, S., Hinings, B. and Ranson, S. (1983) Central–local linkages: the impact of policy planning systems. *Journal of Public Policy*, **3**, 419–34.

Smith, A. (1776) *An Inquiry into the Nature and Causes of the Wealth of Nations*. Republished 1970. Harmondsworth: Penguin.

Smith, W.O. Lester (1945) *To Whom Do Schools Belong?* Oxford: Blackwell.

Smith, W.O. Lester (1965) *The Government of Education*. Harmondsworth: Penguin.

Spens Report (1938) *Secondary Education with Special Reference to Grammar and Technical Education*. London: Consultative Committee of the Board of Education.

Stewart, J. (1977) *The Management of Influence*. Luton: Local Government Management Board.

Stewart, J.D. (1980) From growth to standstill. In M. Wright (ed.), *Public Spending Decisions: Growth and Restraint in the 1970s*. London: Allen & Unwin.

Stewart, J.D. (1983) Local authority. *Times Higher Educational Supplement*, 27 May.

Stewart, J.D. (1984) Tying hands in the town hall. *Times Educational Supplement*, 9 December.

Stillman, A. (1986) *The Balancing Act of 1980: Parents, Politics and Education*. Slough: NFER.

Stillman, A. and Maychell, K. (1986) *Choosing Schools: Parents, LEAs and the 1980 Education Act*. Windsor: NFER–Nelson.

Sullivan, F.B. (1980) *Lord Butler: The 1944 Act in Retrospect*. Milton Keynes: Open University.

Tawney, R.H. (1931) *Equality*. London: Unwin.

Taylor, C. (1985) *Philosophy and the Human Sciences: Philosophical Papers 2*. Cambridge: Cambridge University Press.

Taylor, C. (1989) *Sources of the Self: The Making of Modern Identity*. Cambridge: Cambridge University Press.

Taylor, C. (1991) *The Ethics of Authenticity*. Cambridge, MA: Harvard University Press.

Taylor, C. (1992) *Multiculturalism and 'The Politics of Recognition'*. Princeton, NJ: Princeton University Press.

Thomas, H. (1988) Pupils as vouchers. *Times Educational Supplement*, 2 November.

Thomas, H. (1989) Local management of schools. In B. Cosin, M. Flude and M. Hales (eds), *Schools, Work and Equality*. Sevenoaks: Hodder & Stoughton.

Times Educational Supplement (1982) Church schools in a secular age: what for? (editorial). *Times Educational Supplement*, 22 January.

Titmuss, R.M. (1971) *The Gift Relationship: From Human Blood to Social Policy*. London: Allen & Unwin.

Tomlinson, J. (1988) Curriculum and the market: are they compatible? In J. Haviland (ed.), *Take Care Mr Baker!* London: Fourth Estate.

Trow, M. (1977) The second transformation of American secondary education. In J. Karabel and A.H. Halsey (eds), *Power and Ideology in Education*. New York: Oxford University Press.

Tweedie, J. (1986) Parental choice of school: legislating the balance. In A. Stillman (ed.), *The Balancing Act of 1980: Parents, Politics and Education*. Slough: NFER.

Vaizey, J. (1958) *The Costs of Education*. London: Allen & Unwin.

Vaizey, J. and Debeaurais, M. (1961) Economic aspects of educational development. In A.H. Halsey, J. Find and C. Arnold Anderson (eds), *Education, Economy and Society: A Reader in the Sociology of Education*. London: Macmillan.

Walford, G. (1992) *Selection for Secondary Schooling*. London: National Commission on Education.

Walker, R. (1985) Is there a service economy? The changing capitalist division of labour. *Science and Society*, **49**, 42–83.

Walsh, K. *et al.* (1984) *The Management of Teachers*. Slough: NFER.

Walton, B. (1988) The impact of the Government's legislation upon local government. *Local Government Studies*, **14** (1), 83–91.

Weaver, T. (1979) *Department of Education and Science: Central Control of Education?* Milton Keynes: Open University.

Weber, M. (1978) *Economy and Society*. Berkeley: University of California Press.

Weiner, M. (1981) *English Culture and the Decline of the Industrial Spirit*. Cambridge: Cambridge University Press.

White, J. (1982) *The Aims of Education Restated*. London: Routledge & Kegan Paul.

Whitty, G. (1989) The New Right and the national curriculum: state control or market forces? *Journal of Education Policy*, **4** (4), 329–41.

Williams, G. (1979) Educational planning past and present. *Educational Policy Bulletin*, **7** (2), 125–39.

Williams, R. (1961) *The Long Revolution*. Harmondsworth: Penguin.

Wilson, J. (1985) Render unto Sir Keith. *Times Educational Supplement*, 19 July.

Winkler, J. (1977) The corporate economy: theory and administration. In R. Scase (ed.), *Industrial Society*. London: Allen & Unwin.

Name Index

Subject Index

individualism
  competitive 92
  possessive 91–2, 95
influence 22–3
information 57, 74, 75–6
infrastructure 116–17
in-service development 122
inspection 85, 118; *see also* HMI
institutions 77, 88
  autonomy 88
  rationalization 61
  reform 89–90
integrated curriculum 49–51, 53
investment 6–7, 8

justice 111, 112

Keohane Committee (Report 1979) 45–6, 48
knowledge 4, 5, 49–50

labour market 8
Labour Party 29, 41
learning 120
  active 127, 129
  process 4, 5
    reform 125
  social conditions for 109–10
  vision of 122
  see also child-centred learning
learning self 107–8
learning society
  key components of theory 106–7
  reforming government for 113–29
    central structure 115–19
    local structure 119–24
    organizing principles 113–15
  towards 105–13
LEAs (local education authorities) 20–2, 28, 30, 31, 32, 58–9
  advisory services 59
  and comprehensive reorganization 29–30, 119
  demise 1, 76, 89
  future role of 119, 121, 122–4
  marginalization, 1991 80–6
  and 1944 Education Act 24–5
  and 1980 Education Act 74–5
  and performance 60
  and post-war reforms 119
  and 16–19 policy 57
life, unity of 108
lifestyles 39–40
LMS (local management of schools) 79, 80, 82, 85, 88, 120
local community involvement 26, 127–8
local government 29–30, 119–24
  case for 120
  demise 86–9
  1960s 26
  see also LEAs
Local Government Act (1966) 27

Macfarlane Committee (Report 1980) 57, 60–1, 62–3, 64, 65

management, local, *see* LMS
manpower 6–7
Manpower Services Commission *see* MSC
Mansell Committee (Report 1979) 45–6, 64
market place 70–2
  versus democracy 89–90
  in education 39–40, 69–100
    formation 77
    machinery 91–9
  polity, and civil society 97–9
minimal state 70, 71
Minister of Education 19–20, 21–2, 24–5
moral order 5–6, 11, 16, 39–40, 68–9, 98–9, 105, 109–10, 129
motivation 127
MSC (Manpower Services Commission) 7, 64, 66

National Curriculum 1, 79–80, 84–5
  and Assessment Council 116
  basic standards model 87
  evaluation and monitoring 119
natural selection 94, 98–9
NCVQ (National Council for Vocational Qualifications) 83
neoclassicism 70
networking, and partnership 123, 124, 129
New Society 28
Norwood Report (1943) 27

oil crisis (1973) 37
Omega File (Adam Smith Institute) 75, 76
open enrolment 77
openness 110
opportunities, *see* equality of opportunity
opting out 78, 81, 88, 92
  incentives 82
  see also grant-maintained schools
oversupply 66

PALs (planned admission limits) 74
parent, duty of 22
parent, partnership with 127–8
parent power (parentocracy), *see* parental choice
parental choice 72, 75, 77–80, 87–8, 93, 95
  and cultural capital 95
  and 1980 Education Act 73–5
  planning for 113–14
parents 128–9
Parent's Charter 73, 85
participation, organizational mechanisms 128–9
partnership 22–3, 114, 119
  constituting government as 18–19
  and networking 123, 124, 129
  with parents and community 127–8
performance 60
personal development 8, 10, 11, 17–18, 32, 105, 129
persuasion 56–7
phronesis 106–7
Plowden Committee (Report 1967) 4–5, 10
policy 98
  national 115, 117